PEOPLE YOU KNOW

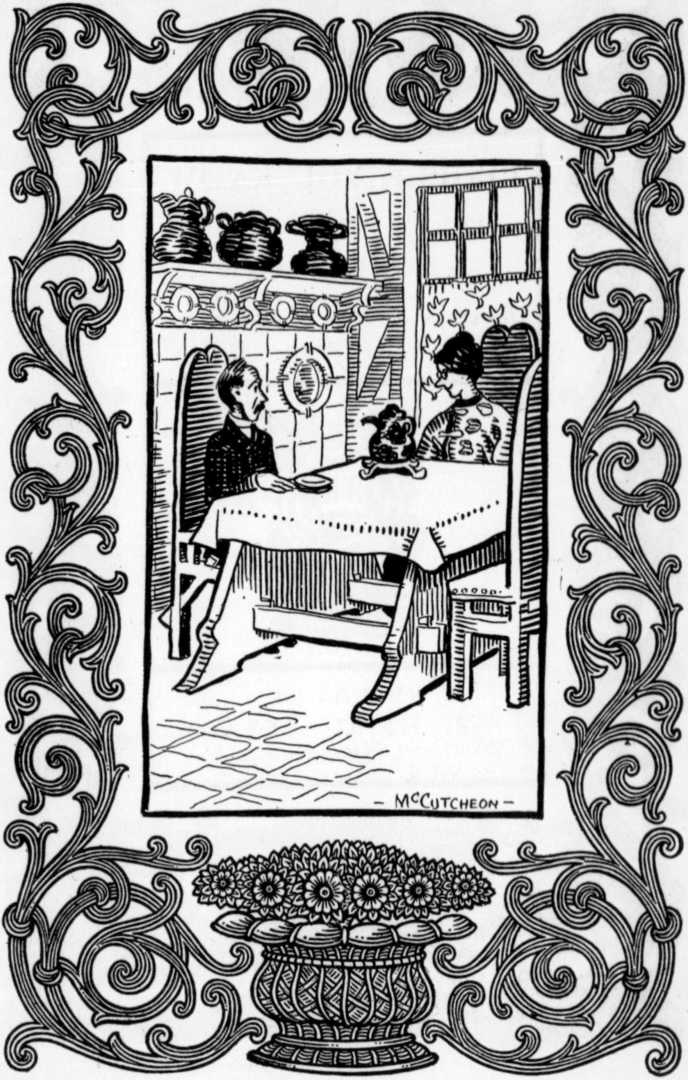

- McCUTCHEON -

PEOPLE YOU KNOW

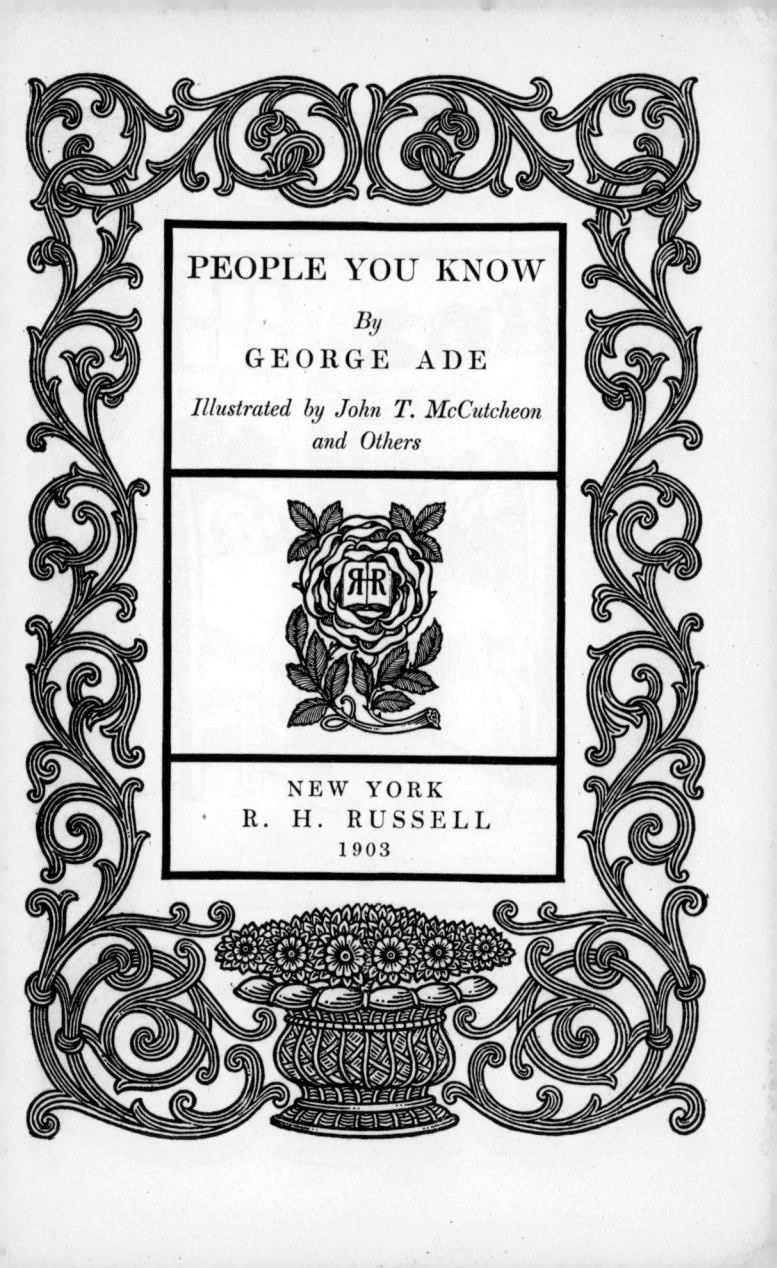

By

GEORGE ADE

*Illustrated by John T. McCutcheon
and Others*

NEW YORK
R. H. RUSSELL
1903

*Copyright, 1902, 1903, by
Robert Howard Russell*

First Impression, April, 1903

The Crow Press, New York

Preface

THIS little book is not supposed to contain any new information. It is made up of plain observations concerning people who live just around the corner. If the reader will bear in mind that *only* the people who live around the corner are discussed in this volume, there will be no chance for painful misunderstandings. I have no desire to rub the wrong way anyone who proves his true friendship by purchasing a copy of this Work. It may be advisable to explain that these Fables are written in the colloquial American language. The vocabulary employed is one that has become familiar to the ear, although it is seldom seen on the printed page. In other words, this volume contains a shameless amount of slang. If any part of it is unintelligible to the reader, he should be glad that he has escaped what seems to be an epidemic.

THE AUTHOR.

CONTENTS

	Page
The Periodical Souse, the Never-Again Feeling and the Ride On the Sprinkling Cart	13
The Kind of Music That Is Too Good for Household Use	23
The One or Two Points of Difference Between Learning and Learning How	26
The Night-Watch and the Would-Be Something Awful	37
The Attenuated Attorney Who Rang In the Associate Counsel	46
What Father Bumped Into at the Culture Factory	54
The Search for the Right House and How Mrs. Jump Had Her Annual Attack	65

CONTENTS

	Page
The Batch of Letters, or One Day With a Busy Man	72
The Sickly Dream and How It Was Doctored Up	81
The Two Old Pals and the Call for Help	90
The Regular Kind of a Place and the Usual Way It Turned Out	99
The Man Who Had a True Friend to Steer Him Along	107
The Young Napoleon Who Went Back to the Store On Monday Morning	110
The High Art That Was a Little Too High for the Vulgarian Who Paid the Bills	119
The Patient Toiler Who Got It in the Usual Place	129
The Summer Vacation That Was Too Good to Last	133

CONTENTS

	Page
How an Humble Beginner Moved from one Pinnacle to Another and Played the Entire Circuit	142
The Maneuvers of Joel and the Disappointed Orphan Asylum	149
Two Young People, Two Photographers and the Corresponding School of Wooing	158
The Married Couple That Went to Housekeeping and Began to Find Out Things	167
The Samaritan Who Got Paralysis of the Helping Hand	175
The Effort to Convert the Work Horse Into a High-Stepper	185
The Self-Made Hezekiah and His Message of Hope to This Year's Crop of Graduates	194

CONTENTS

	Page
The Girl Who Took Notes and Got Wise and Then Fell Down	203
What They Had Laid Out for Their Vacation	212
The Experimental Couple and the Three Off-Shoots	215

The Periodical Souse, the Never-Again Feeling and the Ride On the Sprinkling Cart

ONCE there was an Indian who had a Way of putting on all his Feathers and breaking out of the Reservation. For three Weeks at a Stretch he gave a Correct Imitation of the Shining Light who passes the Basket and superintends the Repairs on the Parsonage. He was entitled to a Mark of 100 for Deportment. With his Meals he drank a little Polly. After Dinner he smoked one Perfecto and then, when he had put in a frolicsome Hour or so with the North American Review, he crawled into the Hay at 9.30 P.M.

At last he accumulated a Sense of Virtue that was hard to carry around. He was proud of himself when he counted up the number of days during which he had stuck to the Straight and Narrow. It seemed to him that he deserved a Reward. So he decided to buy himself a little Present, something costing about 15 cents. He picked out a First-Class Place

PEOPLE YOU KNOW

where they had Electric Fans and Pictures by the Old Masters. He poured out a Workingman's Size—the kind that makes the Barkeep stop wiping up and look unfriendly for a Moment or two.

Then he remembered that a Bird cannot fly with one Wing, so he gently raised the Index Finger and gave the Prescription Clerk a Look, which in the Sign Language means, "Repeat the Dose."

It is an Historical Fact that when a Man falls backward from the Water Wagon he always lands in a Crowd. The full Stage Setting, the Light Effects and the Red Fire were all ready to make it a Spectacular Affair. Just after he had mowed away No. 2 and had stopped worrying about the Winter's Coal, he began to meet Friends who were dying of Thirst. Then the atmosphere began to be curdled with High Balls and Plymouth Sours and Mint Smashes, and he was telling a Shoe Drummer that a lot of People who had been knocking him would probably be working for him before the Year was out.

For Three Weeks.

PEOPLE YOU KNOW

Then he found himself in a four-oared Cablet and the Sea became very Rough. There was something out of Whack with the Steering Gear, for instead of bringing up at his Boarding House he found himself at another Rum Parlor. The Man who owned the Place had lost the Key and could not lock up. Here he met several Delegates to a State Convention of a Fraternal Order having for its Purpose the uplifting of Mankind. They wore Blue Badges and were fighting to get their Money into the Cash Register. In a little while he and a red-headed Delegate were up by the Cigar Counter singing, "How can I bear to leave thee?" He put in an Application for Membership and then the next Picture that came out of the Fog was a Chop Suey Restaurant and everybody breaking Dishes.

Soon after, the Lights went out and when he came back to Earth he was lying the wrong way of his Bed with Blue Badges all over him, trying to swallow a Bath Towel, which he afterward discovered was his Tongue. By getting

Brothers.

a Leverage under his Head he managed to pry it up and then he sat on the edge of the Bed and called himself Names. He had nothing left over except the Cards given to him by the Brothers from up State somewhere. He had a dim and sneaking Recollection that he had given his address and Phone Number to the whole Tribe and begged them to look him up.

"Not any more in Mine," said he, as he held a Towel under the Faucet. "Not for all of Morgan's would I look at any more of that Essence of Trouble. I wonder if I'll live through the Morning."

That Day he lived on Bromo and Ice, and the only Satisfaction this Life offered was the Fact that he was a Reformed Man.

On the Second Day he could look at Solid Food without having a Spasm. His Hair stopped pulling and he began to speak to the People he met. When asked to step out for a little while, he lost his Temper and made a little Talk on the Subject, proving conclusively that there was Nothing in it.

Never Again!

PEOPLE YOU KNOW

As he walked homeward in the Dusk he passed the Clubs and Cafés where those who Drank were rounding up and he felt sorry for them.

"Why can't they pass it up, the same as I do?" he asked himself. "Ah, if only they knew how much more Fun it is to be Respectable."

It was an actual Mystery to him that any one could dally with a Dry Martini while there was a Hydrant on every Corner.

On the third Day he was cracking his Whip and begging People to get up on the Wagon with him. And he said it was a Queer Thing, but he couldn't bear the Sight of it.

While on the fourth Evening he confessed to some nice People he met at a Church Social that at one time he had allowed himself to be coaxed into taking an occasional Nip but he reasoned it all out and decided it was a Bad Thing and simply Chopped it right off. They told him it was wonderful how much Will Power he had and asked him if he ever felt the Old Craving coming back on him, and

THE PERIODICAL SOUSE

he said he could see it splashing all around him and not have the faintest Desire to dip in.

He was so stuck on himself that he went around to call on all his Friends who kept it on the Table so that he could wave it to one side and tell how he despised it. He sat there and pitied those who were inhaling it. Every Morning when he arose he would throw kisses to himself in the Glass and exclaim: "Aha! The Head as clear as a Bell this A.M. I'll bet I'm the cleanest and nicest Young Fellow in this Town. Any Girl that picks out a Sober and Steady Man such as I am will certainly be showing good Judgment."

As Narrated at the Beginning, for three weeks he worked hard at the Job of being an Abstainer. And at last he accumulated a Sense of Virtue that weighed over 200 Pounds. He knew that he was entitled to a Reward, so he decided to buy himself a little Present. Just a wee Reminder of by-gone Days and then back to Sarsaparilla. But he fell into a Crowd. There was another State Convention.

PEOPLE YOU KNOW

It had been arranged for him so that he could get a Fresh Start.

MORAL: Life is a Series of Relapses and Recoveries.

The Kind of Music That Is Too Good for Household Use

ONE Evening a little Flock of Our Best People got together at the Home of a Lady who invariably was first over the Fence in the Mad Pursuit of Culture. She loved to fill her Front Rooms with Folks who wore $7\frac{3}{4}$ Hats and read Norwegian Novels that no one else ever heard anything about.

On the Evening already mentioned she had a Cluster of Geniuses on hand. They were expected to Talk for a couple of Hours, so as to work up an Appetite for Neapolitan Ice-Cream and Lady-Fingers. In the course of time they got around to the Topic of Modern Music. All agreed that the Music which seemed to catch on with the low-browed Public was exceedingly punk. They rather fancied "Parsifal" and were willing to concede that Vogner made good in Spots, but Mascagni they branded as a Crab. As for Victor Herbert and J. P. Sousa—back to the Water-Tanks!

They Love It.

MUSIC TOO GOOD FOR USE

A little later in the Game the Conversation began to Sag and it was suggested that they have Something on the Piano. They gathered around the Stack of Music and then Vogner went into the Discard and Puccini fell to the Floor unnoticed and the Classics did not get a Hand. But they gave a Yelp of Joy when they spotted a dear little Cantata about a Coon who carried a Razor and had trouble with his Wife. They sang the Chorus 38 times and the Young Lady wore out both Wrists doing Rag-Time.

MORAL: It is proper to enjoy the Cheaper Grades of Art, but they should not be formally Indorsed.

The One or Two Points of Difference Between Learning and Learning How

IN a Red School-House back in the Web-Foot District, it was the Custom to have a Debate every Friday Afternoon. The much-mooted Question as to which does the greater Damage, Fire or Water, had been carefully gone over by the Squabs. Also who was the heftier Proposition, Napoleon or Washington? But the original Stand-by was as follows: "Resolved, that Education is better than Wealth."

The Corporate Interests got many a Whack here in the Knowledge Works. Most of the Children wanted to grow up and be like Galileo. They claimed that mere Wealth could not purchase Happiness. The only genuine Peace of Mind came from being able to call off the Geological Periods with the Eyes closed.

Here in this little Brain Hatchery were two Kids who were not Mates. One was named

Otis and Bradford.

PEOPLE YOU KNOW

Otis and the other was Bradford, or Brad for Short. Otis was the Boy who took the Affirmative side on Friday Afternoon. Ote firmly believed that Learning was the most valuable Asset that a Man could tuck away. Brad was for the Money End of the Game, but when he got up to make his Talk his Vocabulary would become jammed up and caught crossways in the Flue and teacher would motion him back to his Seat. Otis, however, could tell in well-chosen Phrases why the Scholar was a better and happier Man than the Millionaire and so he always received the Vote of the Judges.

Now, Brad was done up but unconvinced. He could not stand up before the District School and tell why it was good policy to corral the Coin, but he had a secret Hunch that it would be no Disgrace for him to go out and do the best he could. Brad had a bull-dog Jaw and large blood-shot Hands and a Neck-Band somewhat larger than his Hat-Band. He jumped the Stockade when they started to teach him Botany. He weighed 180 and he

LEARNING AND LEARNING HOW

thought he was too large to sit around and count the Petals of the Ox-Eye Daisy when he might be out selling Lightning Rods to the Yaps and making jug-handled Contracts. Accordingly he Dug.

"Bradford is making a great Mistake," said Otis, as he saw his Friend tear from the Institution of Learning. "In order to get a few worldly Chattels right at the jump, he sacrifices his Diploma. I shall be more Foxy. I shall go right on through the High School and then I shall attend College and get a Degree. When I have taken my Degree then I will be the human *It*. My scholarly Attainments and polished Manner will get me past the Door and into the Inner Circle of the Hot Potatoes. As for Bradford, although it is possible that he shall have combed up a little Currency he will be a mere ordinary, sordid Business Man—not one-two-seven when he tries to stack up against one who has just been delivered of a Thesis on the Correlated Phenomena of Unconscious Cerebration.

While Brad was out in the back Townships

PEOPLE YOU KNOW

short-changing the Farmers and buying 8 per cent. Mortgages, Otis was working his way through College and living on Oatmeal except on Holidays and then Prunes. He was getting round-shouldered and wore Specs and was all gaunted up, but he never weakened. He was pulling for the Laurel Wreath of Scholarship, or in other words, the Degree. After humping it for 4 years he passed his final Exam and the Faculty decided that he was a Bachelor of Arts.

That was the Day when he had the Laugh on Brad.

In the meantime, Bradford had been choking various People and taking it away from them. He had four Salesmen under him and had butted into the Firm, but he was still shy on Botany.

Inasmuch as Otis had been one of the brightest Men in his Class he was offered a position as Instructor in the College at a Salary of $55 a Month with a promise of $5 raise at the end of five Years, if he lived. Otis accepted, because the Outside World did not seem to be

M.A.

PEOPLE YOU KNOW

clamoring for his Services, even though he was an Authority on the Mezozoic Period and knew all the Diatomes by their First Names.

Often while he was burning the Midnight Oil and grinding out Jaw-Breakers, so as to qualify for the Master's Degree, he reflected as follows: "It is true that Brad is making it Hand over Fist and wears $6 Shirts and rides in a State-Room on the Pullman, but he is not a Bachelor of Arts. And some day when he is a Multi-Millionaire I can still look down on him, for then I shall be a Master of Arts. I have known since Childhood that Education is more desirable than Paltry Gold. Although the Newspapers and the General Public do not seem to be with me to any Extent, it is better to hob-nob with the Binomial Theorem than to dally with the Champagne Supper."

In due time the Faculty gave the Degree of M.A. to what was left of Otis and still his Ambition was not satisfied. He wanted to land a Doctor's Degree. He knew that any one who aspired to this Eminent Honor had

LEARNING AND LEARNING HOW

to be a Pippin. But he hoped that he could make some Contribution to the World of Thought that would jar the whole Educational System and help him to climb to the topmost Pinnacle of Human Greatness.

Professor Otis did the Dig Act year after year. At the age of 49 he was still M.A. and owned a House with a Mortgage on it. In the Meantime there had been revolutionary Changes in the World of Finance. Everything on Earth had been put into a Pool. Each Smooth Citizen who had something that was of no particular use to him went to work and Capitalized it. Brad closed out his Interests for so much Money that any one else would have been ashamed to take it. Then he and some other Buccaneers went down to Wall Street to have fun with several dignified Gentlemen whom Brad described as Them Fly Eastern Mugs. They succeeded in putting the Skids under a number of Persons who did not care to meet them Socially.

When Brad walked around in his Million Dollar Hut he had to step high to avoid

PEOPLE YOU KNOW

stumbling over Bundles of the Long Green; but he never had made any further headway with his Botany.

It happened one Day that Brad was out Moting and he dropped in at the College where his Boyhood Friend was now the Professor of Dipsicology and Plamazzus.

"This is a likely-looking Plant," said Brad, as he sized up the Campus. "I like to encourage these Joints because they help to keep a lot of Young Fellows away from Business Offices. I find that I have here in my Vest-Pocket a measly $50,000 that I have overlooked in changing my Clothes. Give it to the Main Cheese and tell him to have a Laboratory on me."

When the News got out all the sis-boom-ah Boys gave a Parade in their Nighties. The Faculty called a Special Meeting and made Brad a Doctor of Philosophy.

Next Year he put up for a Gym and they made him a Doctor of Divinity.

The Year Following he handed them a Telescope and became an LL.D.

D.D.—LL.D.—Ph.D.

PEOPLE YOU KNOW

Every time he coughed he was made some new kind of Doctor.

In fact, for a Man with a 6¼ Hat who did not know the difference between the Pistil and the Stamen he was the most learned Thing in Seven States. Professor Otis was crowded into the Ditch. Sometimes he wonders which of the two has the nub end of the Argument that started in the Red School-House.

MORAL: The Longest Way Around is the Shortest Way to the University Degree.

The Night-Watch and the Would-Be Something Awful

ONCE there was a full-sized Girl named Florine whose Folks kept close Tab on her. Any night-blooming Harold who presumed to keep the Parlor open after Midnight heard low Voices in the Hallway and then a Rap on the Door. If Florine put on her Other Dress and went to a Hop then Mother would sit up and wait for her, and 1 o'clock was the Outside Limit. Consequently Florine would have to duck on the Festivities just when everything was getting Good. Furthermore she would have to warn Mr. Escort to behave himself when they drew near the House.

"Nothing doing at the Gate," she would say, warningly. "It's Dollars to Dumplings that the Girl Detective is peeking out to get a Line on my Conduct. She has her Ear to the Ground about four-thirds of the Time and if any one makes a Move, then Mother is Next. If Father takes a Drink at the Club and then

PEOPLE YOU KNOW

starts Homeward on a fast Trolley, Mother knows all about it when he is still three Blocks from the House. What's more, she is a knowing Bird and can't be fooled by Cloves or these little Peppermint Choo-Choos. The only time when Mother kisses Father is when she wants to catch him with the Goods. Look Out! This is our Corner."

As soon as they had landed at the Gate, little Florine would say in loud, clear Tones that would carry as far as the Sitting-Room Window, "Oh, Mr. Gilblitz, I have had a most charming Evening, and I wish to thank you most heartily."

Whereupon the Escort, standing 8 Feet away, with his Concertina Hat in his Hand and the Face in the Moonlight beaming with child-like Innocence, would come back thusly: "It's awfully good of you to say that. Good Night."

After which, Mother was supposed to believe that they had been 8 feet apart all Evening. But Mother was Canny and up to Snuff, with a Memory that reached back at least 25

Florine.

PEOPLE YOU KNOW

Years. These little One-Act Plays under the Window did not throw her off for any part of a Minute. Before Florine turned in she was Cross-Examined and required to tell with whom she had danced, and why and how often and what he said. Occasionally the Daughter worked the Mental Reservation. In other Words, she held out on Mother. She said that she had sat out most of the Numbers, but she admitted going through a Square Dance with the Young Man who passed the Plate at the Episcopal Church.

At which Mother would wink the Off Eye and murmur, "Is that so?" with the Loud Pedal on the "That." Also something about being more than Seven.

One of Florine's Ancestors on Mother's Side happened to be on Earth at the time of the Revolution, and Father often spoke of a Second Cousin who had been in Congress until the District tumbled to him. Because of this Current of Blue Blood racing in her Veins, Florine was supposed to be a trifle Classy and Mother was always afraid that she might get

THE NIGHT-WATCH

Thumb-Marks on the Family Escutcheon. Therefore Florine was forbidden to work up a Calling Acquaintance with any of the Hoi Polloi, which is Greek for Selling-Platers. According to Mother, there were only about 8 Families in Town that really belonged and some of them didn't Belong enough to hurt. Florine found herself cut out of many a Good Time because the Chaperon for the Occasion chanced to be related to some one who had been in the Liquor Business.

Florine was up against it ever so Hard. She had to go out in the Grape Arbor when she wanted to chew Gum, and she kept her Reading Matter under the Mattress. Nearly every high-speed Bachelor in Town had been forbidden the Premises because of the Stories that were going around. The kind that Mother approved were of the Lilac Division with White Puff Ties and their Hair glued down. They talked about Choir Practice and sometimes, when they were sufficiently wrought up, they played Charades.

The only Chance that Florine had to min-

PEOPLE YOU KNOW

gle with the Popular Boys was to go down Town in the Afternoon and just happen to meet one of them at the Ice-Cream Parlor. Florine learned to be quite a Happener. But on the way home she would have to fix up a few Jules Vernes for the Old Lady in the Watch Tower. Mother knew that it didn't take 4 Hours to be measured for a Shirt Waist.

"Wait until I get Married," Florine would say. "I'll make that 20-hour Flyer look like a Steam-Roller. If Mother doesn't let up on me, I'll learn to smoke Cigarettes."

At times she was so Desperate that she was ready to join a Troupe or elope with a Drummer. She wanted to get out among the Bright Lights and hear the Band play. And she knew that she couldn't turn Flip-Flops and break Furniture and play Rag-Time along after Midnight until she had become a Respectable Married Woman. So she had her Distress Signal out and used to drop very Broad Hints, when she was chatting with the Lads who happened to be in the Soda-Water Resort when she dropped in. They liked Florine for Keeps,

The Night-Watch.

PEOPLE YOU KNOW

but when one of them thought of clinching with old Eagle-Eye, the Family Sleuth, he weakened.

Florine would have remained a Dead Card if she had not gone on a Visit to a neighboring City where she bumped into the Town Trifler. He had a Way of proposing to every Girl the first time he met her. It always seemed to him such a cordial Send-Off for a budding Friendship. Usually the Girl asked for Time and then the two of them would Fiddle around and Fuss and Make Up and finally send back all the Letters and that would be the Finish. Florine fooled the foxy Philander. The Moment he came at her with the Marriage Talk she took a firm Hold and said, "You're on! Get your License to-morrow morning. Then cut all the Telegraph Wires and burn the Railroad Bridges."

They were Married, and, strange as it may appear, Mother immediately resigned her Job as Policeman and said: "Thank goodness, I've got you Married Off! Now you can do as you please."

THE NIGHT-WATCH

When Florine found that she could do as she pleased she discovered that there wasn't very much of anything to do except Settle Down. After about seven Chafing-Dish Parties she expended her whole Stock of pent-up Ginger and now she is just as Quiet as the rest of us.

MORAL: Any System is O. K. if it finally Works Out.

The Attenuated Attorney Who Rang In the Associate Counsel

ONCE there was a sawed-off Attorney who had studied until he was Bleary around the Eyes and as lean as a Razor-Back. He knew the Law from Soup to Nuts, but much learning had put him a little bit to the Willies. And his Size was against him. He lacked Bellows.

He was an inconspicuous little Runt. When he stood up to Plead, he came a trifle higher than the Chair. Of the 90 pounds he carried, about 45 were Gray Matter. He had Mental Merchandise to burn but no way of delivering it.

When there was a Rally or some other Gab-fest on the Bills, the Committee never asked him to make an Address. The Committee wanted a Wind-Jammer who could move the Leaves on a Tree 200 feet distant. The dried-up Lawyer could write Great Stuff that would charm a Bird out of a Tree, but he did not have the Tubes to enable him to Spout. When

THE ATTENUATED ATTORNEY

he got up to Talk, it was all he could do to hear himself. The Juries used to go to sleep on him. He needed a Megaphone. And he had about as much Personal Magnetism as an Undertaker's Assistant.

The Runt lost many a Case because he could not Bark at the Jury and pound Holes in a Table. His Briefs had been greatly admired by the Supreme Court. Also it was known that he could draw up a copper-riveted Contract that would hold Water, but as a Pleader he was a Pickerel.

At one time he had an Important Suit on hand, and he was Worried, for he was opposed by a couple of living Gas Engines who could rare up and down in front of a yap Jury for further Orders.

"I have the Law on my Side," said the Runt. "Now if I were only Six-Feet-Two with a sole-leather Thorax, I could swing the Verdict."

While he was repining, in came a Friend of his Youth, named Jim.

This Jim was a Book-Agent. He was as

PEOPLE YOU KNOW

big as the Side of a House. He had a Voice that sounded as if it came up an Elevator Shaft. When he folded his Arms and looked Solemn, he was a colossal Picture of Power in Repose. He wore a Plug Hat and a large Black Coat. Nature intended him for the U. S. Senate, but used up all the Material early in the Job and failed to stock the Brain Cavity.

Jim had always been at the Foot of the Class in School. At the age of 40 he spelled Sure with an Sh and sank in a Heap when he tried to add 8 and 7. But he was a tall Success as a Book Pedler, because he learned his Piece and the 218 pounds of Dignified Superiority did the Rest.

Wherever he went, he commanded Respect. He could go into a strange Hotel and sit down at the Breakfast Table and say: "Please pass the Syrup" in a Tone that had all the majestic Significance of an Official Utterance. He would sit there in silent Meditation. Those who sized up that elephantine Form and noted the Gravity of his Countenance and the fluted Wrinkles on his high Brow, imagined that he

THE ATTENUATED ATTORNEY

was pondering on the Immortality of the Soul. As a matter of fact, Jim was wondering whether he would take Ham or Bacon with his Eggs.

Jim had the Bulk and the awe-inspiring Front. As long as he held to a Napoleonic Silence he could carry out the Bluff. Little Boys tip-toed when they came near him, and Maiden Ladies sighed for an introduction. Nothing but a Post-Mortem Examination would have shown Jim up in his True Light. The midget Lawyer looked up in Envy at his mastodonic Acquaintance and sighed.

"If I could combine my Intellect with your Horse-Power, I would be the largest Dandelion in the Legal Pasture," he said.

Then a Happy Idea struck him amidships.

"Jim, I want you to be my Associate Counsel," he said. "I understand, of course, that you do not know the difference between a Caveat and a Caviar Sandwich, but as long as you keep your Hair combed the way it is now and wear that Thoughtful Expression, you're just as good as the whole Choate Family. I will introduce you as an Eminent Attorney from

PEOPLE YOU KNOW

the East. I will guard the Law Points and you will sit there and Dismay the Opposition by looking Wise."

So when the Case came up for Trial, the Runt led the august Jim into the Court Room and introduced him as Associate Counsel. A Murmur of Admiration ran throughout the Assemblage when Jim showed his Commanding Figure, a Law Book under his Arm and a look of Heavy Responsibility on his Face. Old Atlas, who carries the Globe on his Shoulders, did not seem to be in it with this grand and gloomy Stranger.

For two hours Jim had been rehearsing his Speech. He arose.

"Your Honor," he began.

At the Sound of that Voice, a scared Silence fell upon the Court Room. It was like the Lower Octave of a Pipe Organ.

"Your Honor," said Jim, "we are ready for Trial."

The musical Rumble filled the Spacious Room and went echoing through the Corridors. The Sound beat out through the Open

Learned Colleague.

PEOPLE YOU KNOW

Windows and checked Traffic in the Street. It sang through the Telegraph Wires and lifted every drooping Flag.

The Jurors turned Pale and began to quiver. Opposing Counsel were as white as a Sheet. Their mute and frightened Faces seemed to ask, "What are we up against?"

Jim sat down and the Trial got under way.

Whenever Jim got his Cue he arose and said, "Your Honor and Gentlemen of the Jury, I quite agree with my learned Colleague."

Then he would relapse and throw on a Socrates Frown and the Other Side would go all to Pieces. Every time Jim cleared his Throat, you could hear a Pin drop. There was no getting away from the dominating Influence of the Master Mind.

The Jury was out only 10 Minutes. When the Verdict was rendered, the Runt, who had provided everything except the Air Pressure, was nearly trampled under foot in the general Rush to Congratulate the distinguished Attorney from the East. The Little Man gathered up his Books and did the customary Slink,

THE ATTENUATED ATTORNEY

while the False Alarm stood in awful Silence and permitted the Judge and others to shake him by the Hand.

Moral: An Associate Counsel should weigh at least 200 Pounds.

What Father Bumped Into at the Culture Factory

A DOMESTIC Team had a Boy named Buchanan who refused to Work, so his Parents decided that he needed a College Education. After he got that, he could enter a Learned Profession, in which Work is a mere Side-Issue.

The Father and Mother of Buchanan sent to the College for a Bunk Catalogue. The Come-On Book had a Green Cover and it was full of Information. It said that the Necessary Expenses counted up about $180 a year. All Students were under helpful and moral Influences from the Moment they arrived. They were expected to hit the Mattress at 10 P.M., while Smoking was forbidden and no one could go to Town except on a Special Permit.

"This is just the Place for Buchanan," said his Mother. "It will be such a Comfort to know that Son is in his Room every Evening."

Accordingly Buchanan was supplied with

THE CULTURE FACTORY

six Shirts, two Suits of everything, a Laundry-Bag, a Pin-Cushion, a Ready-Repair Kit and a Flesh Brush, and away he rode to the Halls of Learning. He wrote back that he was Home-Sick but determined to stick out because he realized the Advantages of a College Education. He said his Eyes hurt him a little from Reading at Night and he had to buy a great many Extra Books, but otherwise he was fine and fancy. Love to all and start a little Currency by the first Mail.

After Buchanan had been toiling up the Hill of Knowledge for nearly two Months, and sending hot Bulletins back to the Old Folks, his Father decided to visit him and give him some Encouragement.

"The Poor Boy must be lonesome down there among all those Strangers," said Father. "I'll drop in on him and brighten him up."

So Father landed in the College Town and inquired for Buchanan, but no one had heard of such a Person.

"Perhaps you mean 'Old Buck,'" said a Pale Youth, with an ingrowing Hat. "If he's

PEOPLE YOU KNOW

the Indian you want to see, I'll show you where he hangs out."

The Proud Parent was steered to a faded Boarding House and found himself in a Chamber of Horrors that seemed to be a Cross between a Junk-Shop and a Turkish Corner. Here he found the College Desperado known as "Old Buck," attired in a Bath-Robe, plunking a stingy little Mandolin and smoking a Cigarette that smelled as if somebody had been standing too close to the Stove.

"Hello, Guv," said the Seeker after Truth. "Wait until I do a Quick Change and we'll go out and get a few lines of Breakfast."

"Breakfast at 2 P.M. ?" inquired Father.

"We had a very busy Night," explained Buchanan. "The Sophomores have disputed our Right to wear Red Neckties, so last night we captured the President of the Soph Class, tied him to a Tree and beat him to a Whisper with a Ball Bat. Then we started over to set fire to the Main Building and we were attacked by a Gang of Sophs. That is how I happened to get this Bum Lamp. Just as he gave me

Souvenirs.

PEOPLE YOU KNOW

the knee, I butted him in the Solar Plexus. He's had two Doctors working on him ever since. And now the Freshies are going to give me a Supper at the Dutch Restaurant to-morrow Night and there is some Talk of electing me Class Poet. So you see, I am getting along fine."

"You are doing Great Work for a Mere Child," said the Parent. "If you keep on, you may be U. S. Senator some day. But tell me, where did you get all of these Sign-Boards, Placards, Head-stones and other Articles of Vertu?"

"I swiped those," replied the Collegian. "In order to be a real Varsity Devil, one must bring home a few Souvenirs every Night he goes out. If the Missionaries did it, it would be called Looting. If the Common People did it, it would be called Petit Larceny. But with us, it is merely a Student Prank."

"I understand," said Father. "Nothing can be more playful than to nail a Tombstone and use it for a Paper-Weight."

"Would you like to look around the Institution?" asked Buchanan.

THE CULTURE FACTORY

"Indeed, I should," was the Reply. "Although I have been denied the blessed Privileges of Higher Education, I love to get into an Atmosphere of four-ply Intellectuality and meet those Souls who are above the sordid Considerations of workaday Commercialism."

"You talk like a Bucket of Ashes," said the Undergraduate. "I'm not going to put you up against any Profs. Follow me and I'll fix it so that you can shake Hands with the Guy that eats 'em alive. I'll take you over to the Corral and show you the Wild-Cats. They've been drinking Blood all Morning and are feeling good and Cagey. About 3 o'clock we turn them out into the Arena and let them plow up the Turf."

"Is this a College or a Zoo?" asked the Parent.

"I refer to the Squad," said Buchanan. "We keep about 40 at the Training Table all of the time, so that no matter how many are killed off, we will always have 11 left. We have a Centre Rush who weighs 238, and you couldn't dent him with a Hatchet. We caught him in the Woods north of Town and brought him down here. He is taking a Special Course in Piano Music two hours a Week and the rest of the Time he is throwing Substitutes down and biting them on the Arm."

Buchanan and his trembling Parent sat at the edge of the Gridiron and watched the Carnage for a while. Buchanan explained that it was merely Friendly Practice.

That Evening the Son said: "Father, you can stay only a Little While and I want to give you a Good Time while you are here. Come with us. We are going down to the Opera House to put a Show on the Bum. One of the first things we learn at College is to kid the Troupers. It is considered Great Sport in these Parts. Then, if any one gets Pinched, we tear down the Jail, thereby preserving the Traditions of dear old Alma Mater."

"Does the Faculty permit you to be guilty of Disorderly Conduct?" asked the Parent.

"Any one who goes against the Faculty single-handed is a Fink," replied Buchanan. "We travel 800 in a Bunch, so that when the

Friendly Practice.

PEOPLE YOU KNOW

Inquest is held, there is no way of finding out just who it was that landed the Punch. Anything that happens in a College Town is an Act of Providence. Now come along and see the American Youth at Play."

They found their way to the Temple of Art. When the Chemical Soubrette started in to sing " Hello, Central, give me Heaven," they gave her just the Opposite of what she was demanding. A few Opera Chairs were pulled up by the Roots and tossed on the Stage, merely to disconcert the Artiste. When the House Policeman came he was hurled 30 Feet into the Air and soon after that the Show broke up. The Student Body flocked out and upset a Trolley Car, and then they went homeward in the Moonlight singing, "Sweet Memories of College Days, La-la! La-la!"

Father's Hat was caved in and he was a trifle Bewildered, but he managed to observe that the Boys were a trifle Boisterous when they got a Fair Start.

"Oh, yes; but they don't Mean anything by it," explained Buchanan.

Preserving the Traditions.

PEOPLE YOU KNOW

"I hope they will explain that to the House Policeman as soon as they get him to the Hospital," said the Parent. "Otherwise, he might misconstrue their Motives."

Next Day, when he went back, he told Mother not to worry about Buchanan, as he seemed to have a full and sympathetic Grasp on the true Inwardness of Modern Educational Methods.

MORAL: Attend to the Remittances and Son will do the Rest.

The Search for the Right House and How Mrs. Jump Had Her Annual Attack

◆§§◆

ONCE there was a Family called Jump that had sampled every Ward within the Corporation Limits.

The Jumps did a Caravan Specialty every time the Frost went out of the Ground.

When the Sarsaparilla Ads began to blossom, and the Peach Crop had been ruined by the late Cold Snap and the Kids were batting up Flies in the Lot back of the Universalist Church, and a Barrel-Organ down Street was tearing the Soul out of "Trovatore"—these were the Cues for Mrs. Jump to get her Nose into the Air and begin to champ at the Bit.

Mother was a House-Hunter from away back. She claimed to be an Invalid eleven months out of the Year and took Nerve Medicine that cost $2.00 a Bottle. Just the same when April hove into view and Dame Nature began to stretch herself, then Mother put on

PEOPLE YOU KNOW

her Short Skirt and a pair of Shoes intended for a Man and did a tall Prance.

She was good for 12 hours a Day on any kind of Pavements. With her Reticule loaded full of "To Let" Clippings, she hot-footed from Street to Street. Every time she struck a Fresh Trail she broke into a Run.

Mother was looking for a House that had twice as many Closets as Rooms and a Southern Exposure on all four sides.

She had conned herself into the Belief that some day she would run down a Queen Anne Shack that would be O. K. in all Particulars.

In the Magazine that came every Month she had seen these Dream-Pictures of Palaces that can be put up for $1,500.00, if you steal your Materials.

She had gazed at the Bunco Illustration of the swell Structure with bushy Trees dotting the Lawn and a little Girl rolling a Hoop along the Cement Side-Walk and she had set her Heart on that kind of a Home.

Mother loved to study the Plans and count the Bath-rooms and figure on Window Seats

May 1st.

and what kind of Curtains to put in the Guest Chamber.

Every Spring she found the Place she had been seeking and gave a Grand Signal for the whole Outfit to begin packing up. Those were the bright vernal Days when Mr. Jump got all that was coming to him. Mr. Jump was a Man, therefore any old kind of a Hut suited him. For eight years before starting on his continuous Tour with Mother, he had roomed over a Drug Store.

His Apartment had been one of those delectable Man-Joints where Women never butted in to hide things and give the whole Place a Soapy Smell.

The Sweepings went under the Bed, so as not to litter up the Hallway.

Once a Year he had a House-Cleaning. That is to say, he employed a Colored Man to beat the Rugs, which had to be separated from the Floor by means of a Shovel.

Inasmuch as Women never came in to straighten up, he knew where to find everything. He knew it was somewhere in the

THE SEARCH FOR A HOUSE

Room and all he had to do was to excavate until he found it.

Then he hooked up with Laura so as to get a real Home and she gave him a new one every Year.

Mr. Jump soon discovered that, although every Man is the Architect of his own Fortune, the Wife usually superintends the Construction.

When Mrs. Jump made her Spring Announcement that they would move to another House, he did a deal of Kicking, but he always went into the Wood Shed to do it. He sassed her inwardly, but not so that she could hear.

She was a Wonder at framing up Reasons for hurling the Lease back at the Landlord.

One Year she quit because the Owner papered the Upstairs with a Jay Pattern that cost only 15 cents a Bolt. Another time the Family next door kept Chickens. Usually the Children across the Alley were not fit Associates for their own little Brood.

One Time she quit on account of a Cockroach. She saw it scoot across the Pantry

PEOPLE YOU KNOW

and that afternoon she headed for a Renting Agency.

Father suggested that instead of vacating in favor of the Cockroach, they offer a reward of $100 for its Capture, dead or alive, and thereby save a little Money, but she refused to listen.

If the Plumbing wasn't out of Whack, the Furnace required too much Coal or else the Woman across the Street had been divorced too many times.

If they squatted in a low-down Neighborhood, Mrs. Jump was ashamed to give her Address to Friends in the Congregation.

If they got into a Nest of the New Rich, then Laura had the freeze-out worked on her, because Mr. Jump was on a Salary and she had to ride on the Trolleys. So she began looking for a Street in which Intellect would successfully stack up against the good, old Collateral. And, of course, that meant a long Search.

Therefore, every May 1st, something Red and about the size of a Caboose backed up to the Jumps'. Several husky Boys began throwing Things out of the Windows.

THE SEARCH FOR A HOUSE

Father did a Vanishing Act. When it came to lifting one corner of a Piano or hanging Pictures he was a sad Bluff and he knew it.

"How about Paradise?" he asked one day. "I understand that inside of the Pearly Gates, each Family has Permanent Quarters. There are no Folding Beds to juggle down Back Stairways, no Picture Cords to Shorten, no Curtain Poles to saw off, no Book Cases to get jammed in Stairways. I am sure there will be no Piano Movers, for I have heard their Language. Do you think you can be happy in the Promised Land?"

"It will depend entirely on whether or not the Rugs fit," she replied.

"Let us hope for the Best," said Mr. Jump.

MORAL: The Queen of the May is usually a Woman.

The Batch of Letters, or One Day With a Busy Man

ONE Morning an energetic little Man who had about a Ton of Work piled up on his Desk came down Town with a Hop, Skip and Jump determined to clean up the whole Lay-Out before Nightfall.

He had taken eight hours of Slumber and a cold Dip in the Porcelain. After Breakfast he came out into the Spring Sunshine feeling as fit as a Fiddle and as snippy as a young Colt.

"Me to the Office to get that Stack of Letters off my Mind," said the Hopeful Citizen.

When he dashed into the Office he carried 220 pounds of Steam and was keen for the Attack.

A tall Man with tan Whiskers arose from behind the roll-top Desk and greeted him.

"How are you feeling this Morning?" asked the Stranger.

"Swell and Sassy," was the Reply.

THE BATCH OF LETTERS

"And yet, to-morrow you may join the Appendicitis Colony and day after to-morrow you may lie in the darkened Front Room with Floral Offerings on all sides," said the Stranger. "What you want is one of our non-reversible, twenty-year, pneumatic Policies with the Reserve Fund Clause. Kindly glance at this Chart. Suppose you take the reactionable Endowment with the special Proviso permitting the accumulation of both Premium and Interest. On a $10,000 Policy for 20 Years you make $8,800 clear, whether you live or die, while the Company loses $3,867.44 as you can see for yourself."

"This is my——" began the Man.

"Or, you may prefer the automatic tontine Policy with ball-bearings," continued the Death Angel. "In this case, the entire Residue goes into the Sinking Fund and draws Compound Interest. This is made possible under our new System of reducing Operating Expenses to a Minimum and putting the Executive Department into the Hands of well-known New York Financiers who do not seek Pecuni-

PEOPLE YOU KNOW

ary Reward but are actuated by a Philanthropic Desire to do good to all Persons living west of the Alleghenies."

"That will be about all from you," said the Man. "Mosey! Duck! Up an Alley!"

"Then you don't care what becomes of your Family?" asked the Stranger, in a horrified Tone.

"My Relatives are collecting all of their Money in Advance," said the Man. "If they are not worrying over the Future, I don't see why you should lose any Sleep."

So the Solicitor went out and told every one along the Street that the Man lacked Foresight.

At 9.30 o'clock the industrious little Man picked up letter number 1 and said to the Blonde Stenographer, "Dear Sir."

At that moment the Head of the Credit Department hit him on the Back and said he had a Good One. It was all about little Frankie, the Only Child, the Phenom, the 40-pound Prodigy.

In every large Establishment there is a

The New House.

PEOPLE YOU KNOW

gurgling Parent who comes down in the Morning with a Story concerning the incipient Depew out at their House. It seems that little Frankie has been told something at Sunday School and he asked his Mother about it and she told him so-and-so, whereupon the Infant Joker arose to the Emergency and said: and then you get it, and any one who doesn't laugh is lacking in a Finer Appreciation of Child Nature. The Busy Man listened to Frankie's Latest and asked, " What's the Rest of it ? "

So the Parent remarked to several People that day that the Man was sinking into a crabbed Old Age.

At 10 A.M. the Man repeated " Dear Sir " and a Voice came to him, remarking on the Beauty of the Weather. A Person who might have been Professor of Bee-Culture in the Pike County Agricultural Seminary, so far as make-up was concerned, took the Man by the Hand and informed him that he (the Man) was a Prominent Citizen and that being the case he would be given a Reduction on the Half-Morocco Edition. While doing his 150 Words a

THE BATCH OF LETTERS

Minute, he worked a Kellar Trick and produced a large Prospectus from under his Coat. Before the Busy Man could grab a Spindle and defend himself, he was looking at a half-tone Photo of Aristotle and listening to all the different Reasons why the Work should be in every Gentleman's Library. Then the Agent whispered the Inside Price to him so that the Stenographer would not hear and began to fill out a Blank. The Man summoned all his Strength and made a Buck.

"I don't read Books," he said. "I am an Intellectual Nit. Clear Out!"

So the Agent gave him a couple of pitying Looks and departed, meeting in the Doorway a pop-eyed Person with his Hat on the Back of his Head and a Roll of Blue Prints under his Arm. The Man looked up and moaned. He recognized his Visitor as a most dangerous Monomaniac—the one who is building a House and wants to show the Plans.

"I've got everything figured out," he began, "except that we can't get from the Dining Room to the Library without going through the Laundry and there's no Flue connecting with the Kitchen. What do you think I'd better do?"

"I think you ought to live at a Hotel," was the reply.

The Monomaniac went home and told his Wife that he had been insulted.

At 11.30 came a Committee of Ladies soliciting Funds for the Home for the Friendless.

"Those who are Friendless don't know their own Luck," said the Busy Man, whereupon the Ladies went outside and agreed that he was a Brute.

At Noon he went out and lunched on Bromo Seltzer.

When he rushed back to tackle his Correspondence, he was met by a large Body of Walking Delegates who told him that he had employed a non-union Man to paint his Barn and that he was a Candidate for the Boycott. He put in an Hour squaring himself and then he turned to the Stenographer.

"How far have we got?" he asked.

"'Dear Sir,'" was the Reply.

The Committee.

PEOPLE YOU KNOW

Just then he got the Last Straw—a bewildered Rufus with a Letter of Introduction. That took 40 Minutes. When Rufe walked out, the Busy Man fell with his Face among the unanswered Letters.

"Call a Cab," he said.

"The 'Phone is out of order," was the Reply.

"Ring for a Messenger," he said.

She pulled the Buzzer and in 20 minutes there slowly entered a boy from the Telegraph Office.

The Man let out a low Howl like that of a Prairie Wolf and ran from the Office. When he arrived at Home he threw his Hat at the Rack and then made the Children back into the Corner and keep quiet. His Wife told around that Henry was Working too hard.

MORAL: Work is a Snap, but the Intermissions do up the Nervous System.

The Sickly Dream and How It Was Doctored Up

❧§§❦

ONE Day a pure white Soul that made Sonnets by hand was sitting in his Apartment embroidering a Canto. He had all the Curtains drawn and was sitting beside a Shaded Candle waiting for the Muse to keep her Appointment. He wore an Azure Dressing-Gown. Occasionally he wept, drying his Eyes on a Salmon Pink Handkerchief bordered with yellow Morning Glories. Any one could tell by looking at him that he was a delicate Organism and had been raised a Pet.

Presently he put his left Hand to his Brow and began to indite with a pearl-handled Pen on Red Paper. Then there was a Ring at the Bell.

"Oh, Fudge!" said the Author. "That distressing Sound! And just when I was beginning to generate Ethereal Vapor. Hereafter I shall order the vulgar Tradespeople to deliver all Marshmallows at the Servants' Entrance."

He began to write again, reviving himself at the end of each Word, by means of Smelling Salts. He did not see the Artist standing in the Doorway.

The Artist was a muscular Person with an Ashen Complexion and a Suit that was not large enough to show the entire Pattern. He carried a Bludgeon with a Horse's Head on it. In order to attract the Attention of Mr. Swinburne, he whistled through his Teeth, whereupon the Author jumped over the Table and fell among the Rugs, faintly calling "Mother! Mother!"

"Cut it out!" exclaimed the Artist. "What's matter? Huh?"

"Oh, how you startled me," said the Author sitting up among the Rugs. "Just as you came in I was writing about the Fays and the Elfins. I was in the deep Greenwood, the velvet Sward kissing my wan Cheek and the Leaves whispering overhead."

"I see," said the Artist. "A Dark Change

The Author.

PEOPLE YOU KNOW

from an Interior to a Wood Set. That's all right if you can do it quick. Who did you say you was doing it for—the Fays?"

"I mentioned the Fays and Elfins," replied the Author.

"I've heard of the Fays," said the Artist. "They're out on the Orpheum Circuit now. But the Elfins—no. What kind of a Turn do they do?"

"Ah, the Elfins!" said the Author. "They dance in the Moonlight and skip from Tree to Tree.

"Acrobatic Stuff with Light Effects, eh? Well, you're on a couple of Mackerels. I never see any Benders that could get away with a Talking Act. You want to give your Piece to somebody that can Boost you. You write a good gingery Skit for me and Miss Fromage and we'll put your Name on a Three-Sheet in Letters big enough to scare a Horse."

"I gather from the somewhat technical Character of your Conversation, my dear sir, that you are associated with the Drama," said the Author.

THE SICKLY DREAM

"Is it a Kid?" asked the Artist. "Wuzn't you ever in Front? Don't you look at the Pictures in the Windows? I'm Rank, of Rank and Fromage. Miss Fromage is the other half this Season, and if you seen her a Block off you'd say, 'Is it or ain't it Lillian Russell?' We've just closed with McGoohan's Boisterous Burlesquers. We was so strong that we killed the rest of the Bill, so we got the Blue Envelope. Now they're using all our Business, including the Gag about the Custard Pie."

"To what am I indebted for the Honor of this Visit?" asked the Author.

"I heard that you was a Litry Mug and I'm around here to see you about a Sketch for me and Miss Fromage. The one I've got now is all right, but in it I've got to eat 8 hardboiled Eggs, and with 4 shows a Day that's askin' too much of any Artist. This Sketch was wrote for us by the Man that handles the Transfer Baggage at Bucyrus. He fixed it up while we was waitin' for a Train. I've been using it since 1882 and it goes just as strong

PEOPLE YOU KNOW

as ever, but I like to get new Stuff once in a while. So I want you to fake up something that'll kill 'em right in their Seats. Here's the Scenario: My Wife's a Society Girl and I'm supposed to be a Dead Swell that's come to take her to a Masquerade. With that to work on, all you need to do is to fill in the Talk."

"I have recently prepared a One-Act Play, but I am not sure that it will meet your Requirements," said the Author. "It is called 'The Language of Flowers.' There are three Characters in the Play—a young Shepherd named Ethelbert, the Lady Gwendolin and a Waiting Maid."

"We couldn't carry three People," said the Artist. "You'd better use a Dummy instead of the Hired Girl. I do an awful funny Wrassle with a Dummy. Go ahead and slip me the Plot."

"It is an idyllic Thing," said the Author. "Ethelbert is in love with Gwendolin, but he is not certain that his Love is reciprocated. So he sends her the Flowers. The waiting-

THE SICKLY DREAM

maid brings them into the Bower where Lady Gwendolin is seated and with them a Scroll of Verses from Ethelbert. The Lady Gwendolin unrolls the Scroll and reads:

" 'Traced in the Veins of the Petals
 Are the Lines I fain would speak
 And breathing low in the perfumed Leaves
 Is the Name——' "

"Hold on," said the Artist. "That's a Cinch. Have a Stage-Hand come on with the Flowers. Lottie says, 'I know who sent these,' and so on and so on, and his Nobs gets off. Then her alone with the big arm-load of Hollyhawks, that I'm supposed to be sendin' her—savvy? She says, 'Well, there's no three ways about it, I've got this Gazabo dead to Rights.' She goes on to talk about Me, leading up to her song, 'John L. will be our Champion once again.' Bing! The Door-Bell rings. Then me on quick, see? I've thought out a Make-Up that's sure to get a Holler the Minute I come on. I wear a pair of Pants made out of

PEOPLE YOU KNOW

Tin Foil, a Fur Coat with Lace around the Bottom and on my Head I wear a Coal-scuttle with some Sleigh-Bells fastened to it. As I come down Stage I make some crack about just escapin' from a Business College. When I see the Doll, I go over and slap her on the Back, pull out a Sprinklin' Can and water the Flowers. You'll have to fix me up a Line to introduce the Sprinkler. As soon as she sees me, she gets stuck, so she hands me one of the Flowers. I say, 'Ah, a night-blooming Pazizum'—then I take a Salt-Cellar out of my Vest and shake some Salt on the Flower and eat it. I done that with a Piece called 'A Boiled Dinner,' and it always went big. When she sees me eat the Flower, that makes her sore, understand? She comes at me with a right-hand Pass. I fall over a Chair and do a Head Spin. You fix up a strong Line for me just as I go over the Chair. Then—What's the matter, Cull? Here, Bud, open your Eyes!"

The Author had fallen in a Heap on the Antique Writing Desk.

THE SICKLY DREAM

"Hully Chee!" exclaimed the Artist. "He's Croaked."

MORAL: A Classic is never Safe Except in the Church Parlor.

The Two Old Pals and the Call for Help

ONCE there was a Married Man who had two Friends whom he had not given up, even to oblige the Missus. They were two Men whom he had known since Boyhood's Happy Days away back in Sleepy Hollow. Once in a while the Man would have the Two around to the House for Dinner.

Of these two Friends, one was a Gusher and the other a Grouch.

The Gusher was eternally bubbling over with Compliments and Kind Wishes. Whenever he met an Acquaintance he handed him a rhetorical Yard of Daisies and then smeared him with Sweet Endearments. His talk never had any specific Purport. It was unadulterated Con. The Gusher should have been in the Diplomatic Service. One of his hot Specialties was to get up at Dinner Parties and propose Toasts. He would hot-air the Ladies until they flushed Crimson from the Joy of being hot-aired. Even if the Speech was known to be cut-and-

The Gusher.

PEOPLE YOU KNOW

dried Blarney, it never failed to swell the Adorable Creatures, as he called them.

He had a pump-handle Shake for every Man he met, and after the second Day he called him Old Fellow and inquired as to his Health in a Tone of trembling Solicitude and picked little pieces of Lint off his Coat.

"I know it's Guff," the Man would say after the Gusher had passed on, "but my Stars! He can ladle out that Soothing Syrup and never spill a Drop."

The Grouch, on the other Hand, gave a correct Imitation of a Bear with a Sore Toe. His Conversation was largely made up of Grunts. He carried a Facial Expression that frightened little Children in Street Cars and took all the Starch out of sentimental Young Ladies. He seemed perpetually to carry the Hoof-Marks of a horrible Nightmare. Some said that he had been Blighted in Love and had soured on the Universe. Others imagined that his Liver was out of Whack. At any rate, he was shy on Sweetness and Light. His Dial suggested a Map of the Bad Lands and he was just out of

THE TWO OLD PALS

Kind Words. He could Knock better than he could Boost.

When the Gusher would arise at the Dinner Table to blow Bubbles and distribute Candy, the Grouch would slide down in his Chair until he was resting on his Shoulder Blades. He seemed to have a Calomel Taste in his Mouth as he listened to the musical drip of the Mush-and-Milk. That kind of Language went with some People, but nix for Sweeney!

The Wife of the Married Man liked the Gusher and tolerated the Grouch.

Every time the Gusher came into the Flat, he held her Hand a little longer than necessary and looked into her Hazel Eyes and told her she was becoming Younger and more Charming every Day. After a Woman turns the 30 Corner, those Speeches are worth a Dollar a Word, because she finds herself Guessing at times. Husband never was jealous. He knew that the Gusher told every Woman the same thing, playing no Favorites.

When the Grouch came to see them, he said "How are you?" and then began to kick on

PEOPLE YOU KNOW

the Weather and tell about his Rheumatism. One thing was certain. The Grouch never would break up any Happy Homes. And it was predicted that he would never get a Wife unless he took her on a Mortgage.

Every Husband has a few Friends who come in for hard Raps from the Wife. And the Grouch got all that was coming to him. She used to declare up and down that she was going to break his Plate and revoke his License. Husband would remind her that he and the Grouch had roomed together at College and done the Comrades Act ever since they were Boys. He would assure her that the Grouch was a Good Fellow, but you had to know him thirty or forty years before you found it out. He would smooth her down and straighten out her Feathers and she would agree to give the Grouch just one more Chance.

It came about that one Year the Married Man got Gay and swam out to where it was over his Head. In his keen Anxiety to enlarge his Business he took on about three Tons of Liabilities. Ninety days make but a fleet-

The Grouch.

PEOPLE YOU KNOW

ing Span when Notes are falling due. One day the Married Man found himself hanging on the edge of the Gully, with a Choice of jumping to the Rocks below or waiting to be Scalped. It was not a dignified thing to do, but he had to yell for Assistance and yell plenty.

He hot-footed to the Gusher, friend of his Youth and God-Father to his Children. He explained that his Heels were beating a Tattoo on the Ragged Edge of Insolvency, and unless he could raise the Wind, it meant a Receiver over at the Works, his Credit evaporated and the Pianola to the Hock-Shop.

The Gusher listened with Tears in his Eyes. In a Voice all choked with Sobs he tendered his Sympathy and his Sincere Hope that all would yet be Well. He told him it grieved him to see a Friend go under the Rollers. It tore his Heart. It did for sure. In fact it had so upset him that he would have to go out into the Air. So he did an Olga Nethersole Exit with one Hand over his streaming Eyes, and the life-long Friend sat there with Salt Water

THE TWO OLD PALS

spattered all over him and nothing in his Hand.

As soon as he had dried his Clothes he went to the Grouch and candidly owned up that he was on the Waiting List for the Poor House unless he could borrow enough to tide him over.

As might have been expected, the Grouch began to Roast him. He told him that he didn't have as much Business Gumption as a Belgian Hare and a Chump who would walk into Debt with his Eyes open deserved to get it right in the Collar.

"If you're looking for Sympathy, you've barked up the wrong Tree," said the Grouch.

"I'm not," was the Reply. "I've just received enough Sympathy to last me all Winter."

The Grouch snarled and reached for his Check Book.

"You can have whatever you need, but you don't deserve it," he said, and he signed it, leaving it Blank above.

"In view of the Fact that you have saved

THE TWO OLD PALS

my Life, I will try to forgive you for lacerating my Feelings," said the Married Man.

They retained the Flat, but the Grouch is just as Unpopular as ever.

MORAL: A Friend who is very Near and Dear may in Time become as useless as a Relative.

The Regular Kind of a Place and the Usual Way It Turned Out

ONCE there was a home-like Beanery where one could tell the Day of the Week by what was on the Table.

The Stroke Oar of this Food Bazaar had been in the Business for 20 years, and she had earned her Harp three times over. The Prune Joke never touched her, and she had herself trained so as not to hear any sarcastic Cracks about the Oleo. She prided herself on the Atmosphere of Culture that permeated the Establishment, and on the Fact that she did not harbor any Improper Characters. A good many Improper Characters came around and sized up the Lay-Out and then blew.

It was a sure-enough Boarding-House, such as many of our Best People know all about even if they won't tell.

The Landlady was doing what she could to discourage the Beef Trust, but she carried a heavy line of Oatmeal. She had Oatmeal to burn and sometimes she did it. And she often

PEOPLE YOU KNOW

remarked that Spinach had Iron in it and was great for the Blood. One of her pet Theories was that Rice contained more Nutriment than could be found in Spring Chicken, but the Boarders allowed that she never saw a Spring Chicken.

In the Cast of Characters were many of the Old Favorites. There was the lippy Boy with the Williams and Walker Shirts, who knew the Names of all the Ball-Players and could tell when there was a good Variety Show in Town.

Then there was the other kind, with a straw-colored Mustache and a prominent Adam's Apple, who was very careful about his Pronunciation. He belonged to a Social Purity Club that had a Yell. His Idea of a Hurrah was to get in a Parlor with a few Sisters who were under the Age Limit and sing the Bass Part of "Pull for the Shore."

Then there was the Old Boarder. He was the Land-Mark. Having lived in Boarding-Houses and Hotels all his Life, he had developed a Gloom that surrounded him like a Morning Fog. He had a Way of turning

The Lippy Boy.

PEOPLE YOU KNOW

Things over with his Fork, as if to say, "Well, I don't know about this." And he never believed anything he saw in the Papers. He said the Papers printed those things just to fill up. The Circassian Princess that brought in the Vittles paid more attention to him than to any one else, because if he didn't get Egg on his Lettuce he was liable to cry all over the Table Cloth.

Then there was the chubby Man who came in every Evening and told what had happened at the Store that Day, and there was a human Ant-Eater who made Puns.

One of the necessary Features of a refined Joint is the Slender Thing who is taking Music and has Mommer along to fight off the Managers and hush the Voice of Scandal. This Boarding-House had one of these Mother-and-Child Combinations that was a Dream. Daughter was full of Kubelik and Josef Hoffman. Away back in the Pines somewhere there was a Father who was putting up for the Outfit. Mother's Job seemed to be to sit around and Root. She was a consistent little

The Old Boarder.

PEOPLE YOU KNOW

Booster. If what Mother said was true, then Effie's Voice was a good deal better than it sounded. She said the Teachers were just crazy about it and all of them agreed that Effie ought to go to Paris or Milan. The slangy Boy with the rag-time Shirt went them one better, and said that *all* of the phoney Melbas in the country ought to pull for the Old Country and wait until they were sent for.

In this same Boarding-House there was a Widow whose husband had neglected to die. Being left all alone in the World she had gone out to make her Way, since which time she had gained about 30 pounds and was considered Great Company by the Young Men.

Necessarily there was a Pale Lady who loved to read, and who stuck to the Patterns that appeared in Godey's Magazine soon after the War.

Then there was the Married Couple, without any Children or Furniture of their own, and the only reason they didn't take a House was that Henry had to be out of Town so often. Henry's Salary had been whooped $500 a

THE REGULAR KIND OF A PLACE

Year and she was just beginning to say Gown instead of Dress. She had the Society Column for Breakfast and things looked Dark for Henry.

For many months this conventional Group of ordinary $6\frac{7}{8}$ Mortals had lived in a Rut. At each meal-time they rounded up and mechanically devoured what was doled out to them and folded their Napkins and broke Ranks. Each day was the Duplicate of another and Life had petered down to a Routine.

One Evening just as they had come in for their Vermicelli, a new Boarder glided into their midst. She was a tall Gypsy Queen with about $1,200 worth of Clothes that fit her everywhere and all the time, and she had this watch-me kind of a Walk, the same being a Cue for all the other Girls to get out their Hardware.

When she moved up to the Table and began to distribute a few sample Smiles, so as to indicate the Character of her Work, the musical Team went out with the Tide, the Grass Widow curled up like an Autumn Leaf, the touch-me-not Married Lady dropped into the Scrub Division. The Lady who read was shy a Spoon and afraid to ask for it. The Men were all google-eyed, and the Help was running into Chairs and dropping important parts of the Menu.

Presently the Landlady came in and explained. She said that Mrs. Williams was in the City to shop for a couple of Days, and her Husband would be up on the Night Train. Whereupon five men fell under the Table.

MORAL: Nothing ever happens at a Boarding House.

The Man Who Had a True Friend to Steer Him Along

ONCE there was a well-meaning Soul who was handicapped by a true and lasting Friendship.

Sometimes he suspected that if he could be left to himself he would struggle along from one Saturday Night to another and keep out of the Way of the Cars and possibly extract some Joy from this Life in his own Simple Rube Fashion.

But every time he turned around, Friend was right there to tell him what to do.

Friend was somewhat of a Shell-Fish in the regulation of his own Private Affairs, but he knew just how to manage for some one else.

So he used to tell the Victim where to have his clothes made, and he would pick out his Shirt Patterns for him and tell him how often he needed a Drink, and in other ways relieve him of all Responsibilities.

If the poor Mark wanted to remain in his Room and read something by William Dean

The True Friend.

THE TRUE FRIEND

Howells, the Friend would compel him to put on his Low-Front and go out to a War-Dance and meet a Bunch of Kioodles who wore No. 6 Hats and talked nothing but Piffle.

The Friend was always making Business Engagements for him and then letting him know about it later on.

And sometimes Friend would try to choke him and take his Money away from him and invest it in some shine Enterprise that was going to pay 40 per cent Dividend every thirty Days.

Friend always meant well at that. When he selected the Girl that the Victim was to marry he was prompted by the most unselfish Motives. Notwithstanding which, the Victim did the tall Duck.

A Policeman found him hiding under a Bridge and asked, "Are you a Fugitive from Justice?"

"No," was the Reply. "This is merely a case of Friend."

MORAL: They never seem to be properly Thankful for all that we do in their Behalf.

The Young Napoleon Who Went Back to the Store on Monday Morning

ONCE there was a feverish Sure-Thinger who started for the Track with a Roll about the size of a Lady's Pencil. He wanted to parlee a $2 Silver Certificate and bring home enough to pay the National Debt.

When he stayed at home and marked the Card and made Mind Bets he could beat five out of six. He estimated that he was losing a Thousand a Month by fooling around the Store when he might be out at the Merry-Go-Round showing the Ikeys how to take a Joke.

And now Saturday Afternoon had come and Percy M. Piker was hanging on the rear end of the Choo-Choo with $7 sewed up in the inside Pocket of his Vest, while in his Hand there fluttered a batch of Clippings, written by the Smoke Brothers, showing which ones were sure to win unless something happened.

Mr. Piker, the amateur Gam, closed his Eyes and saw himself buying a real Panama and a dozen or so George H. Primrose Shirts. He

THE YOUNG NAPOLEON

had a Vision of riding in a Machine called the Pink Demon, with Claire at his side and an imported Chiffonier working the Jigger and mowing down the Common People.

Percy had two or three Good Things that were guaranteed to go through. They had been slipped to him by a Cigar Salesman who knew an Owner. They looked to be the real Candy.

When he arrived at the Track he gave up for a Badge and a Dope-Sheet and a couple of Perfectos, and this left him with 5 and a little something on the side for Red Hots. He fought his way to the Black-Board and demanded $2 worth of Bright Eyes at 9 to 1. While he was struggling to get to the Fence he heard some one say that Appendicitis was right and would win by a City Block. A Low Moan escaped him. He climbed over a large mass of Colored People so as to get $3 down on Appendicitis. The Odds were 7 to 5. He got balled up in his Arithmetic, and while he was waiting for the Figures to shift so that he could butt in with his 3, a Bell rang and the

PEOPLE YOU KNOW

Mob tore for the Fresh Air. He climbed a Pole and saw Bright Eyes doing a Solo. He let go and fell in a Faint. Bright Eyes had beaten the Gate and spread-eagled his Field. It was a Case of winning on the Chin Strap. Mr. Piker was first in the Line, shaking like a Corn-Starch Pudding. He wanted to cash before the Book failed.

A few Moments later he went out behind the Grand Stand and counted up and found that he had $23. He had the Panama and one Shirt. The still, small Voice said, "Duck!" but he thought of Claire and his coming Vacation. There grew within him a high resolve to clean up the Betting Ring and quit the Mercantile Life.

In the Second Race there was a Brown Mare by High-Low-Dreamy Eyes at 97 with Fogarty up, whatever that meant. He heard a Hickey in a Striped Sweater tell a red-headed Man that Josie Jinks would roll in. Accordingly he gnawed his way up to the Workman with the Pencil and laid Twenty at $3\frac{1}{2}$ to 1. Then he wished that he hadn't, for he met a

Getting Down.

PEOPLE YOU KNOW

Friend who whispered "Sassafras" to him. Also he heard some one say that Josie Jinks was three-legged and a bad Actress. After which he went and put Cold Water on his Head and died several Deaths.

Josie Jinks carried on her Back something just out of the Cradle that had number 3 marked on it. Mr. Piker had his Chin over the Fence and was wondering if any one would gather up his Body and put it on the Train. His Pulse was up to 180 and he couldn't hear the Band play.

He saw them come past the first time. Sassafras had a piece of Daylight between himself and the Bunch. The Boy was going along under Double Wraps with a lot up his Sleeve. Away back in the Pocket there was something with a 3 on it. Percy clung to the Fence and he felt the Chill come up his Legs. Sassafras had them smothered. He heard the Roar behind him and knew that an Awful Thing was being pulled off, but he did not have the Heart to look. As they pounded up the Stretch he lifted a dying Gaze and saw a figure 3 move

"Come On!"

out of the horrible Mix-Up and it was all over but the Cashing.

A bug-eyed Maniac with his Collar to the bad was found wandering hither and thither with $90 in his Left Hand. The Tout had to shake him a couple of times before he came to. The Tout had some Goods of a very superior Quality. In the next Race there was a Collie that had enough Hop in him to convert a Selling Plater into a Reina. It was like making change with a Blind Man. Rinkaboo was the Name. Breathe it softly, as very few were Next.

The Tout said to play it across the Board, forward and back, up and down. He said that Rinkaboo would breeze in, that he would win on the Bit, doing Buck and Wing Steps, that all the others would seem to be Hitched.

So, Mr. Piker allowed the Tout to take him by the Hand, for he was too weak to resist, and together they wandered off into Dreamland. Piece by Piece the happy Sesterces went up. Rinkaboo was played in all the Books, straight, place and to peep. Mr. Piker

THE YOUNG NAPOLEON

found himself up in the Grand Stand holding his Head with one Hand while in the other Hand was a Pinochle Deck, suitable for framing. If Rinkaboo finished at all, Mr. Piker was a Wealthy Person. If he happened in toward the head of the Procession, Mr. Piker would have to send for a Furniture Van. If he came First, it would be a case of Hoboken for every Book inside of the Fence.

After it was all over and Mr. Percy M. Piker was riding homeward with his Head out of a Trolley Window, he recalled dimly that a large number of long-legged Ponies came out on the Track. One of them was the color of an Old Glove and was doing a Two-Step. There was about twenty minutes of Fussing around at the Bend in the Track and then they all kited away like a flight of Swallows and there was one Horse in front and Mr. Piker had a Convulsion and frothed at the mouth. Presently the Tonic seemed to die away and something Blew and Rinkaboo fell down and stepped on his Lip. He came in about the time they were blowing the Horn for the next Race.

PEOPLE YOU KNOW

And now Mr. Piker can take Callers up to his Room and tell them how he stood to win $1,340.

MORAL: Even the Best cannot pick them **every** Whirl out of the Box.

The High Art That Was a Little Too High for the Vulgarian Who Paid the Bills

❧§§❧

ONCE there was a Husband who was stuck on Plain Living and Home Comforts. He would walk around an Angel Cake any old Time to get action on some Farm Sausage. He was not very strong for Romaine Salad or any Speckled Cheese left over from Year before last, but he did a very neat vanishing Act with a Sirloin Steak and he had the Coffee come right along in a large Cup. He refused to dally with the Demi-Tasse. For this true American the Course Dinner was a weak Invention of the benighted Foreigner. When he squared up to his Food he cut out all the Trimmings.

This is the kind of Husband who peels his Coat in the Evening and gets himself all spread out in a Rocking Chair with a fat Cushion under him.

He loves to wear old Velvet Slippers with

pink Roses worked on the Toes and the Heels run over.

Give him about two Cigars that pull freely and a Daily Paper and he is fixed for the Session.

Along about 10:30, if he can connect with a Triangle of Desiccated Apple Pie and a Goblet of Milk, he is ready to sink back on the Husks, feeling simply Immense.

Now this Husband had a Fireside that suited him nearly to Death until the Better Half began to read these Magazines that tell how to beautify the Home.

Her first Play was to take out all the Carpets and have the Floors massaged until they were as slick as Glass, so that when the Bread-Winner stepped on one of the Okra or Bokhara Rugs he usually gave an Imitation of a Player trying to reach Second.

He told her that he did not care to live in a Rink, but what he said cut very few Lemons with the Side-Partner. She was looking at the half-tone Pictures of up-to-date Homes and beginning to realize that the Wall-Paper, Steel

Artistic Living Room.

PEOPLE YOU KNOW

Engravings and the Enlarged Photographs of Yap Relatives would have to go.

One Day when the Provider struck the Premises he found the Workmen putting Red Burlap on the Walls of the Sitting-Room.

"Why the Gunny-Sack?" he asked. "Can't we afford Wall-Paper?"

"Love of Art is the True Essence of the Higher Life," said the Æsthete, and she began to read a Booklet bound in the same Paper that the Butcher uses when he wraps up a Soup Bone.

"Come again," said the Wage Earner, who was slow at catching these Ruskin Twisters.

"This is Art Burlap and not the kind that they use for sacking Peanuts," explained the Disciple of Beauty. "Above the Burlap will be a Shelf of Weathered Oak, and then above that a Frieze of Blue Jimson Flowers. Then when we draw all of the Curtains and light one Candle in here it will make a Swell Effect."

"I feel that we are going to be very Happy," he said, and then he went out and sat behind

Artistic Dining-Room.

PEOPLE YOU KNOW

the Barn, where he could smoke his Pipe and meditate on the Uncertainties of Life.

Next Day he discovered that she had condemned his Rocking-Chair and the old-style Centre Table on which he used to stack his Reading Matter and keep a Plate of Apples handy.

When he entered the improved and modernized Living Room, he found himself up against a Job Lot of Beauty and no Mistake.

All the Furniture was straight up and down. It seemed to have been chopped out with an Axe, and was meant to hold up Members of the Rhinoceros Family.

On the High Shelf was a Row of double-handled Shaving Mugs, crippled Beer Steins, undersized Coal Scuttles and various Copper Kettles that had seen Better Days.

"At last we have a Room that satisfies every Craving of my Soul," said the Wife.

"I am more than Satisfied," observed the Treasurer. "I am delirious with Joy. My only regret is that an All-Wise Providence did not mould me into a different Shape so that I

Artistic Bed-Chamber.

might sit down in some of these Chairs. What are those Iron Dinkuses sticking out from the Wall?"

"Those are Florentine Lanterns," she replied; "and they are very Roycroftie, even if they don't give any Light."

Next she started in on the Dining-Room.

Rule No. 1 for making Home more Cheerful is to put in a Shelf wherever there is room for one. After which the Shelf is loaded down with Etruscan Growlers and Antique Jugs.

The low-browed Husband could not tell the difference between High Art and Junk.

The female Bradleyite covered the Walls with about 400 Plates, each with a Blue Curly-Cue on it. They looked very Cheap to him until he received the Bill, and then he learned that they were Old Delft and came to $11 apiece.

In fact, after his Wife had been haunting the Second-Hand Places for a while, he learned that any Article which happened to be old and shopworn and cracked was the one that commanded the Top Price.

HIGH ART

She never let up until she had made the whole House thoroughly Artistic.

Her Women Acquaintances would come in, and she would show them the Dark Oak Effects and the Sea-Green Frescoes and the Monastery Settee with the Sole-Leather Bottom in it and the corroded Tea-Pot that she had bought for $95 and the Table Spread made from Overall Material with just one Yellow Poppy in the Middle, and they would have 37 different kinds of Duck Fits and say that it was Grand and that her Taste was simply Faultless. After that she wouldn't care what Husband said.

He was a fairly patient Man, and all he complained of was that when he sat down he dislocated his Spine, while the Brass Knobs wore black-and-blue Spots on him; and the dining-room Table should have had a couple of Holes for him to put his Legs through; and he couldn't find a Place in which to stretch out; and he needed a Derrick to move one of the Chairs; and at Night when the Moonlight came into his Room and he saw all the bummy

PEOPLE YOU KNOW

Bean-Pots lined up on the Foot-Board and the Instruments of Torture staring at him from every corner of the Room, he would crawl down under the Covers and dream of his Childhood Home, with the old-fashioned Sofas and the deep Rocking-Chairs and the big Bureaus that were meant to hold Things and not to look at.

However, he has been unable to arrest the reaching-out after the Beautiful, for only last Week she purchased a broken-down Clock—price $115.

MORAL: There is no Place like Home, and some Husbands are glad of it.

The Patient Toiler Who Got It in the Usual Place

◆᎑᎑◆

ONCE there was an Office Employee with a Copy-Book Education.

He believed it was his Duty to learn to Labor and to Wait.

He read Pamphlets and Magazine Articles on Success and how to make it a Cinch. He knew that if he made no Changes and never beefed for more Salary, but just buckled down and put in Extra Time and pulled for the House, he would Arrive in time.

The Faithful Worker wanted to be Department Manager. The Hours were short and the Salary large and the Work easy.

He plugged on for many Moons, keeping his Eye on that Roll-Top Desk, for the Manager was getting into the Has-Been Division and he knew there would be a Vacancy.

At last the House gave the old Manager the Privilege of retiring and living on whatever he had saved.

"Ah, this is where Humble Merit gets its

Reward," said the Patient Toiler. "I can see myself counting Money."

That very Day the Main Gazooks led into the Office one of the handsomest Tennis Players that ever worked on Long Island and introduced him all around as the new Department Manager.

"I shall expect you to tell Archibald all about the Business," said the Main Gazooks to the Patient Toiler. "You see he has just graduated from Yale and he doesn't know a dum Thing about Managing anything except a Cat-Boat, but his Father is one of our principal Stock-Holders and he is engaged to a Young Woman whose Uncle is at the head of the Trust."

"I had been hoping to get this Job for myself," said the Faithful Worker, faintly.

"You are so valuable as a Subordinate and have shown such an Aptitude for Detail Work that it would be a Shame to waste you on a $5,000 Job," said the Main Gazooks. "Besides you are not Equipped. You have not been to Yale. Your Father is not a Stock-Holder.

His Ambition.

You are not engaged to a Trust. Get back to your High Stool and whatever Archibald wants to know, you tell him."

MORAL: One who wishes to be a Figure-Head should not Overtrain.

The Summer Vacation That Was Too Good to Last

◦§ ◦§

ONCE there was a Wife who gave the Money-Getter a Vacation by going into the Country for a Month. Dearie took her to the Train, and all the way she kept saying that it did not seem just Right to romp away on a Pleasure Trip and leave him Shell-Roaded.

He began to fear that she would Weaken, so he told her that while he was slaving and humping in the City, it would give him sufficient Joy to know that Darling was out in the Woods, listening to the Birds. He insisted that she should stay until she was thoroughly Rested. Of course, he did not dare to make it too Strong. He played the Self-Sacrifice Gag and threw in a Dash of Marital Solicitude, and made an awful Try at imitating one who has been soaked by a Great Sorrow. As the Missus looked at him through her Tears and held his Salary-Hook in hers, little did she suspect that he had framed up a Poker Festival

PEOPLE YOU KNOW

for that Night and already the Wet Goods were spread out on the Ice.

He had told her that he was going to sit up in the Library every Evening and read Macaulay's History of England. By opening the Windows on both sides he could get a nice Breeze from the West. Along about 10 o'clock, if he got Sleepy, he could turn in. Why not?

It was a lovely Time-Table that he had mapped out. He submitted it to Pet before she went away and she put her O.K. on it, even though her Heart ached for him. Breakfast at the strange Boarding-House. A day of Toil interrupted by a small Bunch of Food at the Dairy Lunch.

Then back to the unfamiliar Faces at the Boarding-House.

Then sitting alone in the Gloaming, thinking of the Absent One.

Then an Hour or two in the Library with the jovial Macaulay.

Then to Bed in the lonesome House and Dreams of Sweetie.

Calling Up the Pirate Crew.

PEOPLE YOU KNOW

He gave her a Schedule which she could consult at any time, Day or Night, and thereby find out what he was doing at that Moment. It was just as convenient as sending a Marconi every Hour or so.

He held himself down until the Train had flirted around the Curve, for he knew that she was watching him from the Observation Car. Then he threw his Hat in the Air and began to do Flip-Flops.

"O, I suppose this is Miserable," he said. "I can see a very poor Month ahead of me—yes—not. Me wearing all my Bells and taking a Hurdle every Furlong."

He rushed in to the Telegraph Office and sent a Wire to her, so that it would catch her at the first Station up the Road. It said not to worry and to take a Good Rest and everything was moving along about the same as usual. With Love and Kisses.

After which he went over to the Brewery to see if they would make a Reduction on Wholesale Orders.

Hubby went up street with his Straw dipped

THE SUMMER VACATION

down in Front, the same as the College Rakes wear them, and his Coat was thrown wide open to show the dizzy Pleats. His Cuban Blood was all het up and he told himself that he was 19 years old and never had a Home.

Oh, but he was Nifty. He was out of the Corral and into the Red Clover and nix any Halter and Box Stall for him. At least not for a Month.

It happened that he had the usual number of disreputable Friends. They were All Right, but he did not dare to have them up to the House, because Angel-Face had investigated them and returned True Bills. They were a little too Gamey for Presbyterian Circles, but they fitted right in at any Function where every man takes off his Coat.

Husband began to use the Telephone, and in the course of an Hour he had organized a Pirate Crew that would go as far as you like at any Game from Pitch-and-Toss to Manslaughter.

For when a decent Married Man does start

PEOPLE YOU KNOW

out to find something different from the calm Joys of connubing in a Side Street, he is the Village Limit.

Husband had the whole Shop to himself. He employed a Senegambian who was a good two-handed Worker with the Corkscrew. Then he had $40 worth of Dutch Lunch sent in from the Rathskeller and arranged the Stacks of Reds, Whites, and Blues. He told himself that the only True Enjoyment was found in Bachelor's Hall.

His Hickey Acquaintances came in, showing more or less Stage Fright, as they were not accustomed to seeing Rugs and Tidies. They told him that he had a Swell Joint. After they had been to the Tea a couple of times they began to peel and one of them started some rowdy Work on the Piano. Another backed into a $30 Statuette and put it out of Business and then offered to pay for it, but the Host said it cost only 98 cents at a Bargain Sale.

At 10 P.M. the Wife, who was in Upper Seven, referred to her Time-Table and saw

Instead of Macaulay.

PEOPLE YOU KNOW

Papa sitting by the Student's Lamp, reading Macaulay. She had no way of knowing that Papa had just been strung for a Month's Rent in a Progressive Jack Pot.

In the Morning when Papa arose and looked at the cold Welsh Rabbits and saw the Cigar Ashes all over the Place and when he had a Taste as if he were taking care of a Lap-Robe, the glad Bohemian Existence did not look as Good to him as it had when lighted up the Night before. Especially as he had got the Zoop for some 80 Buckerines.

Still, there is no one case of Remorse that is going to head off a Man who wants to be rejuvenated. He pulled himself together on the Second Day and resumed the Merry Clip and there was nothing doing in the Macaulay Line. Home did not get him until the Lights had winked out in the other Places. He would not leave the Stag Club or the German Garden, until they began putting the Chairs on the Tables.

For the first two Weeks it was immense. In time, however, it struck him that there was a

THE SUMMER VACATION

certain Monotony in spending one's Money on the Night Owls and showing up with the Milkman. The Poker Players were into him and he began to suspect that he needed a Guardian.

Like every other Man who sends his Wife to a Summer Place, he ended his Hurrah by making a few Resolutions and begging her to come Home.

And she will always believe that he did the Macaulay Act every Evening while she was away. Which is just as well.

MORAL: In order to put a true Value on Civilization, one should pace a few Heats with the Indians now and then.

How an Humble Beginner Moved from One Pinnacle to Another and Played the Entire Circuit

A TEAM of Proud Parents had a son named James Henry Guff. On the Day of his Birth the Wind changed and blew in another Direction, Apples fell off the Trees, Chickens went to Roost at Mid-Day. All Nature seemed to have been given a Jolt by the Portentous Event. For James Henry Guff was born to know all the Brands of Human Greatness. Destiny had put a Green Tag on him and nothing could stop him.

When he was only 18 years of age, he was elected Captain of a Volunteer Fire Department, which was a valuable Organization, only when there was a Fire no one could find the Key to the House in which they kept the Hand-Pump. But the Papers began to speak of him as Captain Guff. His Intimates called him Cap. After the Hose Company disbanded, his Title clung to him and it was generally be-

THE HUMBLE BEGINNER

lieved that he had been with Grant at Appomattox.

Not satisfied with a resounding Title, for which those in the Regular Army have to struggle for Years, Captain Guff began to give Lessons on the Flute at 50 cents an Hour, and the first thing he knew he was a real Professor, just the same as if he had gone up in a Balloon or had some trained Horses. Now over at Harvard, where they grow the English Accent, a Student must grind through a long Course, and a Fellowship and an Instructorship before he blossoms into a simon-pure Professor. Which only goes to show that the Real Boy can gain by one stroke of Genius the Renown for which the ordinary Skates must go forth and Rustle.

James Henry Guff at the age of 30 was both a Captain and a Professor, but his insatiable Ambition spurred him to go out and gather other Laurels. So he ran for Justice of the Peace, and was elected the third time he ran, because the other Candidate pulled out. As Magistrate he became custodian of a Law-Book, a Checker-Board, and a stack of Blank Affidavits. Once every three Months or so somebody would levy on a Cow or threaten to Assault, and then the Judge would get a chance to operate his Graft. But he didn't care so much about the Income, so long as he could be addressed as Judge. He allowed his Hair to grow into a long, graceful Cow-Lick that kept falling into his Eyes, and he looked at the Sidewalk meditatively as he went over to the Grocery to get his Fine-Cut. Sometimes, when he was far enough from Home, those who met him and heard him called Judge thought that he was on the Supreme Bench.

In the course of Time he began to crave a Political Job, so he began to stump around in the Interests of the Machine. He drove out to District School-Houses with the American Eagle seated on the Dash-Board of his Buggy, and when he got on the Platform he waved Old Glory until both Arms gave out. All of which went to prove that the Machine should be kept in Power. After he had been spellbinding for a couple of Seasons a Job Printer

Hon. James Henry Guff.

PEOPLE YOU KNOW

conferred upon him the Title of Honorable. Every time there was a Jim-Crow Speaking, then the Hon. James Henry Guff showed up with his Voice in a Shawl-Strap and also a fine Assortment of Platitudes. When the Congressman wrote to him and asked him to get the Swazey County Delegates into Line, he always addressed his letter to the Hon. James Henry Guff and in the Course of Time Guff began to believe.

But a prouder Distinction awaited him. In view of the fact that he had plugged for the Regular Organization and delivered the Goods at the State Convention, he was made a Colonel on the Governor's Staff. It is the Duty of a Colonel on the Governor's Staff to ride in a Pullman Car and take a Ball every time he is touched on the Back. Colonel Guff was a Dream when he got into his $275 Uniform with the Gold Braid rigged all over the Front. He wore a Chapeau similar to the one worn by Napoleon at Austerlitz, but he had on top of it seven Tail-Feathers of the Loo-Loo Bird, which rather laid over anything that Napoleon

THE HUMBLE BEGINNER

ever wore. And when Colonel James Henry Guff in his magnificent Regalia and smoking a ten-cent Cigar, leaned back in an Open Carriage drawn by White Horses and allowed the People to gaze at him, the Grandeur of the Spectacle made one forget the real Horrors of War.

Many of the ardent Admirers of Prof. Guff, and Capt. Guff, and Judge Guff, and Col. Guff believed that he had climbed to the Summit of Greatness when he appeared in his $42 Plume. Not so. One Year the State Militia was to have an Encampment and the Governor gave Col. James Henry Guff the Job of buying all the Beans, Fresh Beef, and other Supplies, because there promised to be a slight rake-off. Officially he was known as the Commissary-General.

Thus it came about that after Years of Endeavor, James Henry Guff, who left the Post a poor and unknown Boy, went under the Wire a real General.

When his Daughters went away to Boarding School and were introduced as the Offspring of Gen. James H. Guff they assumed a Social

PEOPLE YOU KNOW

Leadership. Gen. Guff led the Grand March at a great many Military Balls. At a Banquet costing $8 per Plate he sat at the Right of the Chairman wearing Medals which had been presented to him by the 4th Ward Marching Club. In his Address he always defended the Soldier against unwarranted Attacks and protested against hauling down the Flag at any Time or Place.

If the Government adopted a new Machine Gun, all the Reporters went over and interviewed Gen. James Henry Guff about it. He wrote a Magazine Article on the Mistakes of the British in South Africa and likewise got rid of a few ponderous Opinions on our Policy in the Philippines.

When he died, the Funeral Procession was two miles long. The Family had to erect two Marble Shafts so as to find Room for all of his Titles.

MORAL: True Democracy scorns a Title unless it has a real Significance, with the Reverse English.

The Maneuvers of Joel and the Disappointed Orphan Asylum

AN old Residenter, who owned a Section of Improved Land, and some Town Property besides, was getting too Feeble to go out and roast the Hired Hands, so he turned the Job over to his Son. This Son was named Joel. He was foolish, the same as a Fox. Any one who got ahead of Joel had to leave a 4:30 Call and start on a Lope. When it came to Skin Games he was the original High-Binder.

Joel took the Old Gentleman aside one Day and said to him: "Father, you are not long for this World, and to save Lawyer Fees and avoid a tie-up in the Probate Court, I think you ought to cut up your Estate your own self, and then you will know it is done Right."

"How had I better divide it?" asked the Old Gentleman.

"You can put the whole Shooting-Match in

PEOPLE YOU KNOW

my Name," suggested Joel. "That will save a lot of Writing. Then if any other Relatives need anything, they can come to me and try to Borrow it."

Joel sent for a cut-rate Shyster, who brought a bundle of Papers tied with Green Braid, and assured the Old Gentleman that the Proceeding was a Mere Formality. When a Legal Wolf wants to work the Do-Do on a Soft Thing, he always springs that Gag about a Mere Formality.

Joel and the Shell-Worker moved the Old Gentleman up to a Table in the Front Room and put a Cushion under him and slipped a Pen into his Hand and showed him where to Sign.

After he got through filling the Blank Spaces with his John Hancock, he didn't have a Window to hoist or a Fence to lean on. He was simply sponging on Joel.

This went on for about a Month, and then Joel began to Fret.

"I don't think I am getting a Square Deal," said Joel. "Here is an Ancient Party

Over the Hills.

PEOPLE YOU KNOW

without any Assets, who lives with me Week in and Week out and doesn't pay any Board. He is getting too Old and Wabbly to do Odd Jobs around the Place, and it looks to me like an awful Imposition."

So he went to the Old Gentleman and said: "Father, I know the Children must annoy you a good deal; they make so much Noise when they play House. Sometimes we want to use the Piano after it is your Bed-Time, and of course that breaks your Rest, so I have been thinking that you would be a lot better off in some Institution where they make a Specialty of looking after Has-Beens. I have discovered a nice, quiet Place. You will live in a large Brick Building, with a lovely Cupola on top. There is a very pretty Lawn, with Flower-Beds, and also an ornamental Iron Fence, so that the Dogs cannot break in and bite you. You will be given a nice Suit of Clothes, the same as all the others are wearing, and if you oversleep yourself in the Morning, a Man will come around and call you."

THE MANEUVERS OF JOEL

"In other Words, me to the Poor-House," said the Old Residenter.

"You need not call it that, unless you want to," said Joel. "If you choose, you may speak of it as the Home for Aged Persons who got Foolish with their Fountain Pens."

So Joel put his Father into the Spring Wagon and hauled him over the Hills to the Charity Pavilion, where all the Old Gentleman had to do was to sit around in the Sun looking at the Pictures in last year's Illustrated Papers and telling what a Chump he had been.

But sometimes a Man is not all in, simply because he looks to be wrinkled and doddering. Joel's Father had a Few Thinks coming to him. Although he had been double-crossed and put through the Ropes, he still had a Punch left. He sent for a Lawyer who was even more Crafty than the one employed by Joel and he said to him: "There is a Loop-Hole in every Written Instrument, if one only knows how to find it. I want you to set aside that fool Deed."

PEOPLE YOU KNOW

Next day the Lawyer came for him in a double-seated Carriage and said, "They forgot to put on a Revenue Stamp and so the Transfer is off."

"And do I get all of my Property back again?" asked the Old Residenter.

"You get half and I get half," was the Reply of the Lawyer.

"Give me mine," said the Old Residenter. "I'm from Wisconsin and I want it in the Hand. Whatever I own from this time on, I carry right in my Clothes, and any Relative who separates me from it will have to set his Request to Music." Then he went to a Physician.

"Doc," he says, "they are counting nine on me, but I figure that before I cash in, I have time to spend all that I have. Look me over and tell me how long I would last on a Waldorf diet. I want to gauge my Expenses so as to leave nothing behind for Joel except a Ha-Ha Message and a few Heirlooms."

"If you want to euchre your Family, why

Second Time on Earth.

don't you leave it to an Orphan Asylum?" suggested the Lawyer.

"Nix the Orphan Asylum," said the Old Residenter. "They would bring a million witnesses to prove that I had been out of my Head for 20 years, and I wouldn't be there to contradict them. I learn that by a singular Coincidence, all the Old People who leave their Money to Hospitals and the like are Mentally Irresponsible. In order to prove that I am in my right Senses, I will Blow mine."

So he went to Palm Beach and other Winter Resorts, at which they charge by the Minute, and wherever he went he gave a faithful Imitation of the Cowboy's first Night in Town.

He bought himself a hot Raglan with a Surcingle around it, and a very doggy line of Cravats, and when he went into the Dining-Room he picked out a Table which commanded a View of the Door at which the Girls came in.

All this time Joel was worried. It seemed

THE MANEUVERS OF JOEL

a Sin and a Shame for an Old Man to go around spending his own Money.

The Residenter had so much Fun during his Second Time on Earth that he decided to make it a sure-enough Renaissance, so he married a Type-Writer 19 years old, that he met in a Hotel Lobby, and then Joel did go up in the Air.

When she began to pick out Snake Rings and Diamond Wish-Bones, the Old Gentleman saw that there was no longer any Hope for Joel.

Moral: When buncoing a Relative always be sure that the Knock-Out Drops are Regulation Strength.

Two Young People, Two Photographers and the Correspondence School of Wooing

ONCE there was a lovely Two-Stepper who went to a Swell Hop and there met a Corkerina who had come to visit a School Friend

He gavotted a few Lines with the Lily. They found it very easy to catch Step together and he did an expert Job of Piloting during the Waltz so as not to get her mussed up, and the consequence was that he made a Grand Impression.

Whenever a Debutter goes away to visit a School Friend, she always meets some Local Adonis who looks to her to be about 60 per cent. better than the stock of Johnnies in her own Burg. And after a Nice Girl has had a long and prosperous Run on the Home Circuit and then begins to curl up on the Edges and show signs of Frost, she will find it a very wise Shift to try new Territory and the

The Two-Stepper.

PEOPLE YOU KNOW

Chances are that she will make a Ten-Strike.

To prove that this is no Idle Jest, it can be demonstrated that the marrying Girl usually goes on the Road a while before she closes a Contract.

The Two-Stepper could not forget the Girl from Another Town. She pulled out next Day but he looked up the Address and sent her the Dance Programme that he had found in his Overcoat Pocket. She wrote back that it was Awfully Sweet of him to remember poor little Me and then she asked one or two Questions. That gave him a Hunch, so he bought a new kind of Writing Paper, said to be the Latest Agony, and he wrote a nice Long Letter in which he told her that she was very easy to look at, and that when it came to picking them up and setting them down in the Slow and Dreamy, she made all the other Girls of his Acquaintance look like a Set of Cripples.

She returned the Serve with one of these chummy Epistles, written on all sides of the

THE SCHOOL OF WOOING

Paper, with the P. S. crawling up one Margin like a Pea-Vine. She chucked in a few mushy Extracts from the Oatmeal School of Thought and asked him the Name of his Favorite Poet.

Her Pace was a trifle Swift for Harry J., who had derived his Education from the Sporting Section of the Daily Papers, but he bought a Lover's Guide and a Dictionary and decided to stay in.

The size of it was that little Harry had been Harpooned all the way through. He was the original Sweetheart à la Brochette. He carried with him, Night and Day, a Vision of Her in the $200 Rig that she had flashed on the Night of the Party. It never occurred to him that she could wear any other Costume. He would close his Eyes and try to hear once again the dulcet and mellifluous Tones of that Voice which, to him, sounded as Good as an Æolian Harp moved by gentle Zephyrs within a Bower of Orchids costing $7 each.

So they exchanged Photos.

PEOPLE YOU KNOW

Next to the Miniature painted on Ivory, the Modern Photo is the prize Bunk of the Universe.

A successful Photographer, who has learned the Tricks and made a slight Study of Human Nature, can take a Grass Widow of 48, who is troubled with Wild Hairs and other Excess Ornaments, and by tampering with the Negative, he can make her out to look something like Ethel Barrymore. Then she can send the Picture to her Relations who live a long way off and they will never know the Difference.

The Girl sent Harry a High Art Panel of herself, in which she was looking at something in a Tree, and when he gazed at it, he had a Palpitation and said, "This is better than I thought it was."

He told himself that it would be a Pleasure and a Privilege to walk up to something like that the 1st of every Month and hand it the Envelope.

He got a clean Shave and put on his Other Clothes and went and had himself Taken by

The Artist.

PEOPLE YOU KNOW

an Artist who charged $8 a Dozen—$4 for the Pictures and $4 to square his Conscience.

This Specialist could take any Set of Misfit Features and rearrange them into a Work of Art. He put Harry in front of the Bull's-Eye and scrooged him around so as to blanket the White Wings as much as possible and then he told him to think of Money and look Pleasant.

When the Pictures were delivered, Harry realized for the first time that he was a Beautiful Creature. He sent one to the Girl and wrote that it was a bum Likeness and did not do him Justice, and so on.

In acknowledging Receipt, she cut out the "Dear Mister" and came right at him with "Dear Friend," which gave him such a Stroke of Joy that he did very little Work that Day.

Harry did not have Gumption enough to evolve any deep System for landing a Tid-Bit, but he had accidentally hit upon the Cinch Method.

So long as Courtship consists of send-

THE SCHOOL OF WOOING

ing idealized Cabinets and exchanging Nice Long Letters, there is but little chance of making Miscues. He never drops in of an Afternoon to find her in a Blue Wrapper and drying her Hair and she never catches him smelling of Cigarettes.

When it comes down to close Work in a Parlor, there is always the Risk of having Herbert Buttinsky on hand to make his Party Call. He who tells his Love by U. S. Mail never hears anything about the Third Party. He lives in the sweet Delusion that he has bought up the whole House.

Harry's Letters to the Girl and the Girl's Letters to Harry became more and more on that Order, until at last they began to burn holes in the Mail Bags.

After comparing her Picture with all the Parlor Favorites that he met on his Social Rounds, he realized that she outclassed all other Representatives of her sex.

In her cosy Flat, far away, she had him propped up on the Piano in a Silver-Gilt Frame and featured to beat the Cars. Any

PEOPLE YOU KNOW

one who dropped in to see her was made to understand that he was merely an Understudy, who was being used as a Time-Killer.

She used to write to Harry and tell him about her Callers and what Chumps they were, and then let him draw his own Conclusions as to who was the real white-haired Papa.

Finally Harry took an Overdose of Nerve Food and asked her right out, would she? The answer came back by Wire and the same Day he sent a sealed Express Package containing the Ring.

After which they began to lay Plans to have a Wedding and become better acquainted.

To be continued in our Next.

MORAL: Absence makes the Heart grow foolish.

The Married Couple That Went to Housekeeping and Began to Find Out Things

⤎⧓⤏

ONCE there was a Happy Young Pair, each of whom got stuck on the Photograph of the other and thereupon a Marriage was arranged by Mail.

Shortly after taking the Life Risk, they started in to get acquainted. Up to the time that they moved into the Arcadian Flats and began to take Orders from the Janitor, he never had seen little Sunshine except in her Evening Frock.

He had a sort of sneaking Suspicion that she arose every Morning already attired in a Paris Gown and all the Diamonds.

And she supposed that he went to the Office every Day in his regular John Drew effect with the Folding Hat.

After she began to see Hubby around the Flat in his Other Clothes the Horrible Truth dawned upon her that he was not such a Hot

PEOPLE YOU KNOW

Swell as he had looked to be in the Bunko Photograph.

Sometimes, on Rainy Sundays, he would cut out the Morning Service and decide not to Shave, and then when she got a good long Look at him, she would begin to doubt her own Judgment.

And so far as that is concerned, there were Mornings, after they had been out Late to a Welsh Rabbit Party, when she was a little Lumpy, if any one should ask.

Love's Young Dream was handed several goshawful Whacks about the Time that they started in to get a Line on each other.

For instance, the first Morning at Breakfast it came out that her Idea of a Dainty Snack with which to usher in the Day was a Lettuce Sandwich, a Couple of Olives and a Child's Cup full of Cocoa, while he wanted $35 worth of Ham and Eggs, a stack of Griddle Cakes and a Tureen of Coffee.

She was a case of Ambrosia and Nectar and he was plain old Ham and Spinach.

It used to give her Hysterics to see him

Inhaling It.

PEOPLE YOU KNOW

bark at an Ear of Green Corn, at the same time making a Sound like a Dredge.

For Dinner she liked a little Consommé en Tasse and then a Nice Salad, while he insisted on a Steak the size of a Door Mat and German Fried to come along.

They did not Mocha and Java at all on their Reading Matter. She liked Henry James and Walter Pater and he preferred Horse Papers and the Comic Supplement. Sometimes when she would wander off into the Realms of Poesy he would follow her as far as he could, and then sit down and wait for her to get through rambling and come back.

If they took in a Show she was always plugging for Mrs. Fiske or Duse, while he claimed that Rogers Brothers were better than Booth and Barrett had been in their Prime.

She could weep over a Tosti Serenade, and he would walk a Mile at any time to see a good Buck Dance.

When they got around to fixing up Invita-

THE MARRIED COUPLE

tion Lists, there was more or less Geeing and Hawing.

All of his Friends belonged to the Hitemup Division. Their only Conception of a Happy Evening was to put the Buck in the Centre of the Table, break a fresh Pack and go out for Blood.

Wifey found her most delirious Joy in putting passionate Shades on all the Lamps, and sitting there in the Crimson Glow to discuss Maeterlinck and Maarten Maartens and a few others that were New Ones on the he-end of the Sketch.

When they had an Evening At Home up in the Flat, it was usually a two-ring Affair. She would have the Cerebellums in the Front Room looking at the New Books and eating Peppermint Wafers, while he and the other Comanches would be out in the Dining-Room trying to make their House Rent and tossing off that which made Scotland famous. Sometimes it would take half the Night to get the Smoke out of the House.

Although she feared that she had turned

up the wrong Street while searching for her Affinity, the Partnership Arrangement had to stand.

They came to the Conclusion that Married Life is a Series of Compromises. If he did well while sitting in with some of his Friends, he would divide up with her and she would take the Money and buy Art Pastels.

He would spot the Afternoons on which the Ethical Researchers were due at his Premises and he would go to a Dutch Restaurant.

She permitted him to have a Room and call it his Den, so that he and his Friends could do the Escape in case somebody in the Parlor started a Reading.

He put up the Coin to enable her to attend State Conventions, and when she was elected Recording Secretary of the Society for trying to find out what Browning was up to, he took her Picture around to all the Newspapers and told every one that he had a little Woman up at the House who was as Keen as a Hawk, as Swift as an Eagle, and Sharper than Chained Lightning.

The Comanches.

PEOPLE YOU KNOW

He fumbled a great many of her In-Shoots, but that did not prevent him from admiring her Delivery.

Finally they arranged their separate Schedules so that they did not see much of each other and they began to get along all right. Occasionally they had a slight Difference, but they could always patch it up. For instance, she selected Aubrey De Courcey as a Name for the First Born, while he held out for Bill, so they had to compromise on Aubrey De Courcey.

Aubrey is now ten years of age. Mother is teaching him to Crochet and Father is showing him how to Draw without tipping off his Hand, while all the Friends are sitting around, waiting to see Aubrey's Finish.

MORAL: The Two of a Kind is not always the Strongest Combination.

The Samaritan Who Got Paralysis of the Helping Hand

ONCE there was a moving Target who was strong on the Brotherhood of Man. He ran a little Sunshine Factory all of his own. When it came to scattering Seeds of Kindness, the Farm Drill was a Poor Second.

Every time he started down Town he would have to zigzag so as to cover both sides of the Street and glad-hand all of his Acquaintances.

From time to time he joined Fraternal Organizations and took blistering Oaths that he would always love his Fellow-Man and stand for any Touch within Reason. Consequently a good many People found it cheaper to send for him than to hire a Professional Nurse. He would travel Miles in order to have the Pleasure of sitting up with a Corpse. And he was one of the handiest Pall-Bearers in the Business.

PEOPLE YOU KNOW

Any one who happened to be nursing a Hard-Luck Story would hunt up sympathetic Jasper and give him the Grip and then weep on his Shoulder. Usually he promised to do what he could to square Matters, even though he had to cut in where he wasn't wanted. In flying around, trying to re-instate No-Goods who had lost their Jobs and secure Salaried Positions for Nice Fellows who were willing to do anything except Work, he got many a Jolt, but he was not discouraged.

One of his regular Assignments was to arbitrate a Domestic Scrap, merely out of the Goodness of his Heart.

In this way he managed to re-unite quite a number of Couples who were afterward sorry that they had been reuned, and what they said about him would get the Blue Pencil if inserted at this Point.

When a kind-hearted Herring starts out to be a Relief Bureau and First Aid to the Injured and a portable Home for the Friendless, nobody tries to take the Job away from

A Touch.

him. His Acquaintances do what they can to boost his Game.

Therefore when any one in that Community sought out a Busy Man of Affairs and began to unwrap his Tale of Woe and offer to exhibit his wounds, the B. M. of A. would say, "Here, I'll give you a Letter of Introduction to my old friend Jasper. He is a Samaritan from away back."

It came about that Jasper's Outer Office was frequently coagulated with a Choice Assortment of Pan-Handlers, and all the short-winded Brothers who want to hitch on to somebody's else Pull, as they say in Boston.

At times Jasper would become weary of having Folks come along and turn their Private Griefs over to him, but he did not want to become a Cynic and lose his Faith in Human Nature. He was frequently Stung, but still he could not resist any Appeal that was backed up by a few Weeps.

In the Course of Time he came into quite a Bundle of Money, and then all the Bread that he had cast on the Waters came back to

The Promoter.

PEOPLE YOU KNOW

him, a Bakery at a time. Those whom he had succored came around to Sucker him.

A Promoter whose Schemes he had guaranteed, because the Man's Children needed Shoes, now had a Chance to show his Gratitude. He let Jasper in on the Ground Floor of a Company organized to manufacture an Automobile that could be turned out of the Shop for $35 and would run 90 Miles on a pint of Gasoline.

Gentlemen who were getting along without Overcoats came in to see him about Mining Stock that was sure to touch Par by January 1st. The only Reason they came to him first, instead of tackling John W. Gates, was that he had always been a True Friend and they wanted to put him next to a Good Thing.

After one or two of these Gift Enterprises had been slipped to him, he began to back water and be a trifle Sore. Yet he found it very Hard to be discourteous to one who came in and did the Brother Act. Besides, the Bunk who has the Joint Note already made out and ready to be signed, usually has a Talk

THE SAMARITAN

calculated to make a Heart of Stone mellow to the Consistency of a Baked Apple.

What really did more than any other one Thing to cure him of his Innate Goodness was an Experience with a Sweet Girl who was being courted by a Hound quite unworthy of her.

The unselfish Benefactor who tries to sidetrack Weddings that are sure to turn out unhappily is always a Candidate for the Hospital, with a Long Shot at the Morgue.

The Sweet Girl in Question was the daughter of an Old Friend, for whose Funeral Expenses he had been landed. She was a Confiding Thing, and did not know that the Bachelor who had started in to Rush her seven nights a Week was a Rounder and a Poker-Player and somewhat of a Lush.

Every one who knew the Sweet Girl said it was too Bad and that some one ought to go to her and warn her. After the Old Ladies and the Elders had talked the Matter over on the side, it was decided that Jasper was It. He was known to be kind and disinterested and was accustomed to dealing out Good Advice. Anything that he said would go a long Way to head off the Deal.

Accordingly he did a Fatherly Talk to the Daughter of his Old Friend, giving her a Straight Line on the Conduct of the High-Roller who was trying to warm up to her.

She thanked him right from the Bottom of her heart. Then she sent a Messenger Boy to hunt up the High-Roller, because she wanted to know if it was all True or merely a Cruel Slander.

When she sprung his Record on him he leaned right over against her and cried and said that no matter what he had been, she was the one to make him a Good Man. Then she stroked his Hair and begged Forgiveness and he asked her who had been Knocking and she gave the whole Snap away and begged him not to do anything Desperate. He said that whatever he did, he would do out of Love for her.

After which he went home to oil up his Pocket Hardware.

Fatherly Advice.

PEOPLE YOU KNOW

Next Morning the Man who wanted to help Everybody did a Flying Leap down the Back Stairway of his Office. Just as he ducked a Bullet and cut into the Alley back of the Post-Office, it occurred to him that the True Friend Gag had its Drawbacks.

He escaped with his Life, but there was always more or less Dark Talk of his being mixed up in a Woman Case.

He is now what is known in Obituary Notices as a Practical Philanthropist. That is, he refers all Hard-Luck Tales to a Society which was never known to give up. The Office Boy has Instructions to admit only those who are listed in Bradstreet. And, of course, he is never called in to smooth out Family Fights because of the Blot on his Character.

MORAL: To be a successful Benefactor, wait and put the whole Lump Sum into Libraries.

The Effort to Convert the Work Horse Into a High-Stepper

ONCE there was a plain, unvarnished Yank who made his Pile in a Scrub Town situated midway between the Oats Belt and the Tall Timber. He was a large and sandy Mortal with a steel-trap Jaw and a cold glittering Eye. He made his first Stack a Dollar at a Time on straight Deals, but after a while he learned a few Things. He organized Stock Companies and then crawled out after hooking up with the Velvet. Every one called him Mister and treated him with Politeness, but, just the same, when he walked into an Office Building they all wondered what he had come after and there was more or less locking of Safes. It is only fair to remark, on the Side, that he wouldn't take anything which was securely spiked down, and the Grand Jury never bothered him, because he worked under a Contract.

The Financier was the high Centre Pole of

PEOPLE YOU KNOW

a Bank and a Department Store and several Factories that gave Young People a Start in the World at something like $2.75 per Week.

He was accustomed to having all the Subordinates stand on one Foot and tremble whenever he showed up. In fact, he was a very hefty Proposition all through the Business District. But when he struck the Street leading to his House he began to reef his Sails and lower all of his Flags.

In his own Domicile he did not even play Second Fiddle. He simply trailed along at the fag end of the Parade and carried the Music. The Piercing Eye and the Peremptory Manner that caused all the Book-keepers to fall off from their High Perches and prostrate themselves had no visible effect on Laura and the Girls. Popsy was a High Guy at the Directors' Meeting, but a mighty cheap Soufflé at his own Fireside. Any time that his Plans did not coincide with those of the Feminine Bunch, they passed him a backhanded Veto that would cause him to lie quiet for Days at a time.

Scrub Town.

PEOPLE YOU KNOW

The Financier loved the boundless West, where the Sack Coat abounds and the Cuss-Word is a common Heritage. Domestic Cigars were good enough for him, and he figured that one good reliable Hired Girl who knew how to cook Steak was all the Help that was needed in any House. But Mother had seen Fifth Avenue in a Dream, and the Girls had attended a Boarding School at which nearly every one knew some one who was Prominent Socially. They had done a lot of Hard Work at the Piano and taken a side-hold on the French Language and it seemed to them that they were wasting their Time in loitering on the Outskirts of Civilization when they might be up at Headquarters cutting more or less of a Gash. All the Young Men in this Reub Town wore Derbies with their Evening Clothes and came to Dances with their White Gloves smelling of Gasoline, in addition to which they lacked Repose. If they had stopped to cultivate Repose, most of them would have landed in the Villa set aside for Paupers.

THE WORK HORSE

When Laura and the Girls first advocated pulling up Stakes and doing a tall Hike to the East, the Producer emitted a Roar that would have frightened any one except Laura and the Girls. They closed in on him from three Directions and beat down his Defence. When they got through with the living Meal Ticket he was as meek as an English Servant and ready to take orders from any one.

So the Caravansary moved away toward the Rising Sun. At Wilkesbarre, Pennsylvania, the Heavens opened and a Great Light struck down upon them, transforming all except the one who happened to carry the Letter of Credit. Laura and the Girls suddenly forgot that there was any Land west of Pittsburg, and they dropped their R's and got the Kangaroo Walk and began to order their Food in Foreign Languages. After that, all Father had to do was to follow along and look Pleasant and dig every few Minutes.

The Outfit stopped at the Waldorf three days so as to obtain a Residence, and after that they Registered as being from New

PEOPLE YOU KNOW

York. Then they threw Papa on a Boat and took him to the Other Side, the Place where Americans are so Popular, if you don't care what you say. By paying off the Mortgage they obtained a Suite at a Hotel patronized by the Nobility and Gentry and supported by People from Iowa. After which they began to present Letters of Introduction and try to butt in. Laura and the Girls felt that if only they could eat a Meal once or twice in the gloomy Presence of those who had Handles to their Names, they would be ready to fall back and die Happy. They had some Trouble about getting into the Tall Game on account of their Money. In the States the general Run of People worship the Almighty Dollar, but in England they hate the Sight of it.

In spite of the Fact that they were sinfully Rich they succeeded in Elbowing their way into several Dinners at which it was necessary to put Ice into the Claret in order to keep it at the Temperature of the Room. The Financier, in his First Part Clothes with an Ice-

Laura's Ambition.

PEOPLE YOU KNOW

Cream Weskit, was a Picture that no Artist could paint. His hair would not stay combed and he hardly ever knew what to do with his Hands.

Laura and the Girls could forget that they had once seen the Missouri River, but not so with Old Ready Money. Right at the Table, sitting opposite the Earl of Hammersmith or the Marquis of Stroke-on-Trent, while Laura and the Girls would be talking about their Country Place and trying to smother the American Accent, the Lobsterine would come in and tell about something that happened to him once when he was plowing Corn. Then Laura and the Girls would want to duck right under the Table and die of Mortification then and there.

The only Reason they put up with him was that he seemed to be useful when it came to signing Checks.

In England they met a great many Nice People. The Financier knew that they were Nice because they wore Dark Clothes and seldom Smiled.

THE WORK HORSE

Then the two shapely Daughters went and married a couple of shelf-worn Titles.

The Financier had the Novel Experience of putting up for a Brace of Sons-in-Law who would not speak to him when any one was around. Which served him right, for he had no Business to be in Trade. It was very careless of him not to have inherited his Stuff.

Still, it was a great Satisfaction to him to be a Blood Relative of two Howling Swells who had Pedigrees reaching back almost as far as their Debts.

Very often he would take them into a Back Room and turn them around and look them over and recognize the cold, undeniable Fact that they were cheap at any Price.

MORAL: Bunker Hill has been Avenged, over and over.

Self-Made Hezekiah and His Message of Hope to This Year's Crop of Graduates

IN Wayback Township, along in the Thirties, there arrived a 12-pounder. When he was three days old he was exhibited to a Bunch in the Front Room by an Old Lady who had made a Study of Colic. She was a Baby Expert who always broke in to do considerable heavy standing around and calling off when there was a lift in the Population.

While little Ipsy-Wipsy was being inspected, he opened one Eye and spotted a silver Half-Dollar that the Honorary Nurse wore as a Brooch. Immediately he closed in on it. They had to choke him to make him let go. In after Years it was remarked that this was the only time that he went after the Coin and failed to bring it home.

The Baby never had any Tantrums at Night because he had overheard them say

THE SELF-MADE HEZEKIAH

that it cost $2 every time Doc was called in. He would lie quietly in his Crib for Hours at a time looking up at the Ceiling and computing Compound Interest on the $5 Gold Piece that had been put in the Bank, to be drawn out when he should be 21.

His Parents gave him a Biblical Name so so as to make him a strong Come-On for Investors who belong to the Pious Element. Hezekiah Hooper is what they christened him. They wanted a Name that would carry weight on a Letter-Head and reassure the Soft Mark who was about to sink his Funds in a Mining Venture with a Guarantee of 48 per cent. Dividends.

At the age of 4 Hezekiah sat down and figured that if he devoted his Life to Physical Toil, he might some day be the Owner of a six-room cottage fully protected by a Mortgage, whereas if he wore a White Shirt and kept busy with the Pencil, he might be Rich enough some day to land in the Senate. So he went out looking for Work to hand to other People, thus becoming what

PEOPLE YOU KNOW

the Campaign Orator calls a Captain of Industry.

If a man wanted the Weeds pulled from his Garden, then Hez would take the Job for 25 cents. He would buy 5 cents worth of Stick Candy and place it judiciously, so that at Nightfall the other boys would have Blisters and the Stomach-Ache, while Hez would have 20 cents salted away in the Tin Bank.

When he was still a Young Man he made the Important Discovery that the honest Laborer who digs Post-Holes for 11 Hours at a Stretch gets $1.25 in the Currency of the Realm, while the Brain-Worker who leads out a Spavined Horse and puts in 20 Minutes at tall Bunko Work, can clean up $14.50 and then sit on the Porch all Afternoon, reading "The Lives of the Saints."

Also Hezekiah led up to the Altar a Hold-Over whose Eyes refused to work as a Duet and whose Figure had all of the graceful Ins and Outs of a Flag-Pole, but she owned half of the Land in the Township. Hezekiah said something about the Beauty that fadeth even

[196]

Hezekiah.

PEOPLE YOU KNOW

as a Flower, and then he connected with her Property.

When grim-visaged War showed its awful Front, Hezekiah went down to the Court-House and hollered for the Union until he was black in the Face. He showed all the emotional Farm Hands where to sign their Names and promised to keep them supplied with Blue Overcoats, Beans, Navy Plug and Hard Tack until the whole Works had been saved. Every time there was a new Call for Men, he took a firmer hold on the Commissary Department and began to gouge the Government in a new Place.

The Heroes who came home full of Malaria and Lead were met at the Station by Hezekiah, who had grown a Chin Whisker and was sporting a White Vest. He gave each one a Card announcing that all of our country's Brave Defenders who had failed to become well fixed on $13 per, would get what Money they needed at 2 per cent. a Month, with Real Estate as Security.

By going through Bankruptcy, side-step-

This Year's Crop.

PEOPLE YOU KNOW

ping the Assessor, working the Farmers for a Railroad Bonus, handling the Funds for denominational Colleges and putting the double Hammer-Lock on the Small Fry who had Notes falling due, Hezekiah accumulated a Wad that put him into the Millionaire's Division.

He and other old Gentlemen with pink Jowls and cold fishy Eyes would occasionally meet in some Directors' Room, finished in Mahogany. The Meeting would be opened with Prayer, after which they would discuss Ways and Means of putting the Inter-State Commerce Law to the Bad, squaring the Legislature without passing over any of the Stuff themselves and handing the Public the Short End of it.

Having arrived at this Proud Eminence, Hezekiah was ripe to spring some Advice to Young Men. Any Patriarch who has slipped the Tall Mitt to the entire Universe and dealt from both Ends of the Deck is the Real Boy when it comes to laying down Rules of Conduct for the Pale Youth who wants an $8

THE SELF-MADE HEZEKIAH

Job. So Hezekiah Hooper, the Eminent Financier, who never smoked a Cigar, never took a Drink and never asked anybody else to do either, was invited to address the Class of Naughty-Three at the Local Business College.

He sat on the Rostrum wearing Black Broadcloth, betokening Virtue, and in addition to his ancient Trade-Marks, the White Shirt and the White Vest, he had a White Bow Tie. As he sat there in conscious Rectitude, wondering if the Congressional Investigation would harm the Beef Trust, it could be seen at a Glance that he would never take anything that was too heavy to carry, unless he had a Dray.

The studious Young Gentlemen who had been preparing themselves to go out into the Great World and draw Car-Fare as Book-Keepers and Stenographers, looked up at Honest Hezekiah and said, "This is where he puts us next to the Recipe for Getting There."

At last the Honored Guest arose and told

PEOPLE YOU KNOW

the Class that the Young Man who wishes to succeed must be Upright, Frugal, Industrious, and Patriotic. He considered it the Duty of every Young Man to accept whatever Compensation was offered him and be Content, for as soon as he began to earn more his Employer would come around and put it in his Pocket. Above all, he must love his Country and let Integrity be his Watchword and remember that a Good Name is better than Riches, even if other People don't think so. Then he sat down without batting an Eye and every member of the Class of '03 knew just how to go out and pile up a Million.

MORAL: What's more, they believe it themselves.

The Girl Who Took Notes and Got Wise and Then Fell Down

ONCE upon a Time there was a long-headed Girl who used to sit in her own Room on Rainy Afternoons and evolve Theories. Her principal Ambition in Life was to stand Ace High with all the Nice Men of her Set. She hoped in the course of Time to tease one away from the Drove and gallop him into the Branding Pen.

Now this Girl was so Foxy that at times she got in front of herself and blocked off her own Plays. Her scheme for getting all the Real Boys intoxified with Love for her was to engage them in Conversation and find out what kind of Girls they liked. Then her Play was to be that Kind. She had no Difficulty whatever in inducing her Men Friends to talk about the Opposite Sex. They were all keyed up on the Subject and full of Information. Just as a Feeler one Evening she asked an eligible Charley if he didn't think that the Woman of To-day was too Extravagant.

PEOPLE YOU KNOW

"That's just why so many of us shy at the Matrimonial Jump," he confided to her. "There was a time when the Man who got $75 per Month and had about $200 planted could take a Chance at the Game. But now that measly Allowance wouldn't keep a High Roller supplied with Violets. The up-to-date Maudine isn't happy unless she has a Gray-Squirrel Coat, an Auto Car, $11,000 worth of Twinklers and a fourteen-room Apartment. That's why these Society Shawl-Holders keep on making Love right and left but never come down to Cases."

This was a valuable Tip, so the crafty Maiden put it down in her little Note-Book that she who would make a Hit must convince the Men that her Tastes were simple and inexpensive. Another one gave her a learned Talk on the frivolity and Two-by-Fourness of the typical Seraphine.

"You cannot expect a Man to hand over his serious Affections to one of these Feather-Heads," he said, as he gazed thoughtfully at the Floor. "Woman should be Man's Intel-

Nice Men.

lectual Helpmeet. Now and then a Man may have a Passing Fancy for a Lizzie who talks Piffle and gets an Attack of the Giggles every few Seconds, but when it comes to the grand Hook-Up he wants one who is there with the Gray Matter—one who can play up to his loftiest Ambitions and supply his Home with that Atmosphere of Culture which is the true Ozone of Married Life."

So she put it down that it was her Cue to chop out the Twaddle and be a sort of Lady Emerson. Incidentally she resolved to cut out all kinds of Slang, for she got a very straight Line of Talk from an Amateur Philosopher who was in the Wholesale Grocery Business.

"If there's anything that gives me a quick, shooting Pain it is to hear some delicate Nectarine dealing out Slang," said Mr. Gentleman Friend. "Now in England, where I spent Two Weeks once, the Ladies never use Slang. They simply say that a Thing is either Perfectly Charming or Most Extraordinary and let it go at that. They may be

Rules of Conduct.

PEOPLE YOU KNOW

Short on Vocabulary, but they are Long on Respectability. Besides, I was reading in a Magazine the other Day that Slang is Vulgar and that no one should take up with a Slang Word until Long Usage has given it the right to break into the Lexicon."

Also this Girl with the Absorbent Mind would clip out Hints to the Young, and Confidential Charts warning the Just-Outs against taking Presents from Strangers and putting them next to Rules of Conduct that would be sure to please and fascinate Proper Young Men. It seemed strange at Times that these Head Coaches who knew just how to jolly up any Man were not out spending some Millionaire's Money instead of writing Pieces for the Paper.

All the Articles on the Woman's Page and all the strait-laced Men that she met came down Hard on the Female who is trying to be a Real Bohemian. She learned from a dozen different Sources that Men have no earthly Use for the Zipper who tries to do a Mile in less than Two and kites around in a

THE GIRL WHO TOOK NOTES

Hack without a Chaperon and carries her own Cigarettes.

And she heard nothing but Expressions of Horror concerning the Woman who Drinks. Her Male acquaintances often brought up the Painful Subject. They said it was all right for a Man to move up to a High Ball once in a While, and a Cocktail before Dinner didn't do any Harm until after the Seventh or Eighth. But it did look Tough to see Mere Children of about twenty-three Years of Age going after the Dry Manhattans.

After sounding the Men on the Liquor Question the long-headed Girl made a solemn Resolve that she would never hit up anything stronger than Cherry Sundae.

When she had her Note Book full of useful Directions she found a Chance to try out her System. She was invited to a Swell Dinner Party at which all the Nice Men in Town were to be rounded up. She put on a simple White Gown and wore a Rose in her Hair, and just before starting she locked all of her

PEOPLE YOU KNOW

Slang words in the Escritoire, whatever that may be.

At the Dinner she sat next to a Bachelor who had Nothing But. She talked to him about the Panama Canal, just to show that she was no Piker. When he wanted her to take some of the Phizz Water she made an Awful Stand and seemed surprised that he should think that of her.

This did not prevent him from splashing in. By the time the Birds came along he had accumulated a very neat Brannigan, and was paying a lot of Attention to a wonderful Piece of Work sitting opposite. She wore a Red Costume that must have cost $7,000, and although she was very gabby and called the Men by their First Names and invited all who were not Quitters to stand by for a Bumper, she was making fair Headway. In fact, she seemed to have the Bunch with her.

The Wise Girl figured that they were tolerating her out of mere Politeness. Later on, in the Drawing Room, they continued to tolerate her the best they knew how. The Girl

THE GIRL WHO TOOK NOTES

with the Book of Rules played a sad little Opus on the Piano, after which the Steeple-Chaser in Red leaped on top of the Instrument and tore out Coon Stuff with eight men turning the Music for her.

And these were the Eight who had told the Girl back in the Corner all about the Qualities in Woman that would help to attract Men. She went home thinking it over and the next time she started for a Dinner, she added a Dash of Red and a few Brilliants to the Costume and cut loose up to a reasonable Limit. She got along first-rate, even though she was doing a lot of Things that none of the Men approve, but somehow love to put up with.

MORAL: He can always pick out the Right Kind for the Other Fellow.

What They Had Laid Out for Their Vacation

◦§§◦

A MAN who had three weeks of Vacation coming to him began to get busy with an Atlas about April 1st. He and his Wife figured that by keeping on the Jump they could do Niagara, Thousand Islands, Atlantic City, The Mammoth Cave and cover the Great Lakes.

On April 10th they decided to charter a House-Boat and float down the Mississippi.

On April 20th he heard of a Cheap Excursion to California with a stop-over Privilege at every Station and they began to read up on Salt Lake and Yellowstone.

On May 1st she flashed a Prospectus of a Northern Lake Resort where Boats and Minnows were free and Nature was ever smiling.

By May 10th he had drawn a Blue Pencil all over a Folder of the Adirondack Region, and all the Hotel Rates were set down in his Pocket Memorandum Book.

Ten days later she vetoed the Mountain

Getting Busy With an Atlas.

PEOPLE YOU KNOW

Trip because she had got next to a Nantucket Establishment where Family Board was $6 a Week, with the use of a Horse.

On June 1st a Friend showed him how, by making two Changes and hiring a Canoe, he could penetrate the Deep Woods, where the Foot of Man had never Trod and the Black Bass came to the Surface and begged to be taken out.

On June 15th he and Wifey packed up and did the annual Hike up to Uncle Foster's Place in Brown County, where they ate with the Hired Hand and had Greens three times a Day. There were no Screens on the Windows, but by climbing a Hill they could get a lovely View of the Pike that ran over to the County Seat.

MORAL: If Summer came in the Spring there would be a lot of Travel.

The Experimental Couple and the Three Off-Shoots

A MAN and Wife had three Sons. The first, named Abraham Lincoln Tibbetts, was born in 1862. His name was promptly abbreviated to Link.

The second, who arrived in 1872, was christened Ulysses Simpson Grant Tibbetts. This was too long, so people called him Chub.

The third was of the Vintage of 1882 and his name went into the Register as Chester A. Arthur Tibbetts, but, in the interest of Euphony he was dubbed Art, because Art is Long.

The Tibbetts Family lived in the City, and Link, the first-born, enjoyed all the Advantages of Life in an Apartment Building. He went to a Graded School and picked up so much Knowledge that at the age of 12 he could set his Parents down in front of him and tell them Things they did not know. At 14 he was so far along that he knew how to lie in Bed and have his Mother bring his

PEOPLE YOU KNOW

Breakfast up to him. He went to Dancing School and learned to play all the "Pinafore" music on the Upright Agony Box. Sometimes he chided Mr. and Mrs. Tibbetts for not having as much Money as many of the People he met at Dancing Parties. He had about as much Application as a used-up Porous Plaster, and he worried more about his Complexion than he did about his Business Prospects.

Mr. Tibbetts gave him a Desk at the Office and called him Assistant Something. His Duties consisted of looking at the Clock and writing Notes to the Gazelles he had met the Night before. If he had been set out on the Pavement and told to Root for himself, it would have broken him of the habit of Eating.

Link was whatever they called a Lobster in 1880. Mr. Tibbetts realized that City Life had an enervating Effect on Boys and made them Superficial and Wise in their own Conceit.

Chub was 8 years old and had not yet suc-

Link.

PEOPLE YOU KNOW

cumbed to the Matinee Habit, so his Parents decided to ship him out to the Green Fields and keep him there until he had developed a Character. Mr. and Mrs. Tibbetts knew that all the Men of Sterling Worth, mentioned in Political Biographies, had been raised on the Farm. They figured that if Chub could be left in the Country to run with the Live Stock, he would grow up to be a Sturdy and self-reliant Character, with no hankering for Soda Water and the Military Schottische.

Therefore Chub was sent out to live with Uncle Jabez Quackenbush, an Agriculturalist who owned 480 Acres and was still wearing the Army Overcoat that the Government had given him when the War broke out. Chub slept on a Feather Tick up in a Room where they had the Seed Corn hung on the Rafters. Uncle Jabe would yank him out at 4.30 G. M. and keep him in the Field until the early Candle-Lighting, so that usually he had two Meals in the Dark. On Sunday he and the Hired Help would sit in the Hay-Mow and

Chub.

PEOPLE YOU KNOW

read Almanacs. In the Winter he attended a District School and learned to bound Patagonia, but he did not go to any demoralizing Shows nor learn to pick up flip Slang.

When he was 18, he seemed to be past the Danger Period, so Uncle Jabe took him to the Train and told the Conductor where to put him off. On the way back to the City he bought an oval Box of Figs from the Train Boy and lost his Hat out of the Window. When he arrived at Home and entered the House, it sounded like a Crowd coming in. His Mother took one Look and fell backward. There was a Neutral Zone between his Vest and Trousers. Also he had been raising Warts on himself.

For two Months after he arrived they kept him under Cover for fear the Neighbors would see him. He gave way at the Knees every time he stepped. If a member of the Opposite Sex spoke to him, he usually backed into something Breakable. At the Table he he did a Sword-Swallowing Act and drank out of the Saucer.

THE EXPERIMENTAL COUPLE

"We made a mistake in leaving him so long in the Tall Grass," said Mr. Tibbetts. "But now that we have tried the two Extremes, we know just what to do with Art. We shall send him to a small Town, where he may associate with bright Youth of his own age and yet be away from the distracting and corrupting Influences of the Big City."

Accordingly Art was farmed out to a Cousin residing in a drowsy Corporation of about 1,500 Souls, figuratively speaking. He went to the Grammar School and what he didn't learn at School he learned in Back Alleys and Box Cars. However, his Parents were happy in the Knowledge that he was beyond the influence of the gaudy Play House, the gilded Buffet and the seductive Dancing Academy. He was out where nothing happened unless the Boys started it themselves. So they started it.

When he was twenty he was sent to the City, an extra fine Specimen of what the Small Town can produce. He had his Hair combed down into his Eyes. He wore a punky little Derby, about two sizes too small. The turn-down Collar was four inches high, and he wore a navy-blue Cravat with a copper Butterfly for a Scarf-Pin. Furthermore, he had a Suit of Clothes that was intended for a gentle Brakeman. On his Lapel he had a Button Photograph of the Girl who worked in the Millinery Store.

"Are you made up for a Masquerade or is this the regular Costume?" asked his Father.

" 'Go 'Way Back and Set Down,' " replied Art, for he knew his Village Repartee and was on to all of last year's Gags.

"What do you propose to do for yourself?" asked Mr. Tibbetts.

"I want to travel with a Circus or Minstrel Troupe and I don't much care which," replied Art.

As the Boy appeared to be somewhat Lumpy about the Pockets, his Father threw him down and searched him, finding on his Person, a $2 Revolver, a Package of Cigaroots, a 1-lb. Plug of Tobacco, a Deck

Art.

PEOPLE YOU KNOW

of Playing Cards, a Copy of "Old Sleuth" and a Pair of Brass Knucks.

"I have underrated the Educational Facilities of the Jay Town," said Mr. Tibbetts. "Link is door-keeper in a Dime Museum and Chub is putting in Coal for an old and well-known Firm, but I can see that you are going to outshine your Brothers. You are going to develop into a first-class Burglar."

MORAL: Keep him in a Barrel.

RR
fox